Sea Planes of the Legion Condor

Sea Planes of the

Legion Condor

The Story of AS./88 Squadron in the Spanish Civil War 1936-1939

Rafael Permuy López and César O'Donnell

Schiffer Military History
Atglen, PA

Acknowledgments

This book would not have been possible without the collaboration of a number of individuals and institutions.

The authors would like to express their gratitude to a group of friends, who did not hesitate to offer their advice, data, photographs, drawings, and translations. They are, in alphabetical order: Raúl Arias, Luis Avial, Luis Ignacio Azaola, José M. Campesino, Cristino Castroviejo, Juan Luis Coello, Juan Carlos Díaz Lorenzo, Jacinto García Barbero, Francisco González Huix, José Luis González Serrano, Santiago Guillén, Justo Miranda, Jesús López Morcillo, Lucas Molina, Isabel Ortega, Günther Ott, Peregrín Pascual, Miguel Puchol, Luis Sáenz de Pazos, Juan Carlos Salgado, Franz Selinger, Francisco Javier Sánchez Lladó, Santiago Sánchez Renedo, and Harold Thiele.

We would also like to thank the followong institutions and organizations: The General Maritime Records "Álvaro de Bazán"; The Central Naval Archive; the Avila General Military Archive; the Salamanca Civil War Archive; The Air Force Historical Archive; the Iberisa Archive; the National Library, Madrid; Bundesarchiv Militararchiv Freiburg; the Aeronautical Historical and Cultural Institute; and the Air Force Historical and Cultural Service.

Book Design by Ian Robertson.

Library of Congress Control Number: 2009936436

Printed in China.
ISBN: 978-0-7643-3341-5

This book was originally published in Spanish under the title
Ad de Picas: La Escuadrilla de Hidros de la Legión Cóndor en la Guerra Civil Española (1936-1939) by Galland Books

Contents

Introduction

Among the different *Luftwaffe* units that formed part of the Condor Legion, one in particular stands out for its important Naval Air contribution: the *Aufklärungsstaffel See/88*, better known by the abbreviation AS./88, or the Maritime Reconnaissance Squadron, although it was also officially designated the *Seefliegerstaffel AS./88*, or Naval Air Squadron AS./88.

However, sixty-five years after the end of the Spanish Civil War (1936-1939), one of the least known aspects of the war's tragic history is undoubtedly the Condor Legion's use of sea planes against the merchant marine of Spain's II Republic, both at sea and in port (mainly in the Mediterranean). There were numerous incidents, above all when the targeted vessels were foreign, especially those flying the British or French flag, which in turn led to missions of this type being abandoned for periods lasting several days due to protests made through diplomatic channels.

This resulted in the German seaplanes concentrating their efforts on targets along the coast, such as fuel dumps, factories manufacturing war materiel, roads, convoys, communications, and bridges, as well as locomotives and military trains and railway installations. The effectiveness of the attacks carried out on the last mentioned type of targets earned the crews the epithet "the railway men" at the Condor Legion's headquarters.

One of our main aims in presenting this work has been to avoid falling into the trap of going over ground already covered in previous studies with varying success, which is why our intention is to try and provide until now unpublished aspects regarding the main operations and war service of both the personnel and aircraft of AS./88, which, during a period of three years, participated directly in the Spanish Civil War of 1936-1939 on the Nationalist side.

AS./88 Squadron was to employ the following aircraft during the Spanish campaign:

- Twenty-seven Heinkel He 59 bomber, torpedo, and reconnaissance seaplanes.
- Seven Heinkel He 60 close reconnaissance/bomber seaplanes.
- Two Heinkel He 115 A-0 reconnaissance/torpedo seaplanes.
- A Junkers Ju 52/3 m (W) transport/liaison seaplane (fitted with floats).

Opposite: Only the Heinkel He 60s in service with Spanish squadrons carried the type number 60. The German planes were all numbered from 511 to 515.

1

The Arrival of the First Seaplanes and the Creation of AS./88 Squadron

1.1.- The first German seaplanes to reach Spain

On 14 October, the 4,177 ton passenger ship *Eisenach* (Elize), belonging to Nord Deustcher Lloyd, arrived at the port of Seville carrying six passengers and 329 tons of war materiel plus two single-engine Heinkel He 60s. The aircraft were immediately taken to Puntales (Cádiz), where they were put together and armed at the factory belonging to Construcciones Aeronáuticas Sociedad Anónima (C.A.S.A.), which specialized in constructing Dornier Wal and Vickers Vildebeest seaplanes under license. Among the passengers who had landed with the *Eisenach* were two observers: *Hauptmann* Karl-Heinz Wolf and *Leutnant* Siegmund Storp, as well as two mechanics.

The German merchant ship *Stassfurt* (7,395 tons), belonging to the Hapag shipping company, left Stettin on 19 November and arrived in Seville on the 27th, disembarking

It was not until the end of the war that the three Heinkel He 59s handed over to the Nationalist Air Force were designated 71.

216 passengers, 19 tons of military supplies, and 95 vehicles, together with two twin-engined Heinkel He 59s, which were also put together in Cadiz. These aircraft were also accompanied by two observers: *Oberleutnant* Werner Klümper and Dieter Leicht; plus two pilots: *Oberfeldwebel* Johann Gaessler and *Unteroffizier* Bernhardt Winse.

Finally, on 23 December, 1,257 tons of war materiel, together with another two Heinkel He 60s, were landed from the 1,846 ton German merchant ship *Capri* (Carla), Sloman R.M. of Hamburg. The planes were fitted and equipped in Cádiz, and then taken to the El Atalayón (Melilla) Air Base.

1.2.- The numbering of seaplanes used in Spain.

There has been a lot of conjecture over the numbering of German seaplanes in Spain. The Heinkel He 60s bore the numbers 511 to 515 on the sides of their fuselages, and the first three were baptized "The terror of the seas" (511), "The sea beast" (512), and "The sea wolf" (513). The twin-engined Heinkel He 59s sent to Spain between 1936 and 1937 were numbered 521 to 530, with one exception: that of number 527, which was assigned to the three-engine Junkers Ju 52/3m (W), fitted with floats, and assigned to AS./88 to carry out transportation and liaison tasks, and for which their is graphic evidence.

These correspond to the first type-numbers authorized by the Section responsible for materiel in the staff of the Nationalist Air Force during the month of October 1936. The numbers belonging to the group 50 to 59 corresponded to seaplane fighters. "50" was assigned to the Macchi M. 41, and when the Heinkel He 60s arrived, they had to be considered as seaplanes of the same category and were assigned the number "51." However, when the Germans numbered the aircraft individually they ommitted to place the regulation hyphen which was supposed to separate the type-number from the aircraft's own number, which should have run, for example, 51-1, 51-2, etc.

In so far as the Heinkel He 59s were concerned, given that the Germans acted in an almost independant manner, it is undoubted that they decided themselves that these twin-engined planes should be assigned the number "52," and so painted this type-number on the fuselages, again ommitting the hyphen.

The twin-engined Heinkel He 59s of AS./88 carried the type numbers 521 to 548.

What is certain is that the Air Force Command issued new type-numbers in February 1937 and re-numbered the Heinkel He 60s with the type-number "60" (reconnaissance seaplanes), and the Heinkel He 59s were assigned the number "71" (bombers). Therefore, it should be noted that, during the Spanish civil war, the only German planes complying

Below: *Factorías de Construcciones Aeronáuticas S.A.* (the Aeronautical Construction Factory Inc.) in Cadiz was where the first Heinkel He 60s to arrive in Spain in October 1936 were assembled and armed.

with that regulation were the four Heinkel He 60s ceded to the Nationalist Air Force. As the seaplanes were capable of being launched by catapult from a ship they were handed over to the Navy and assigned to the cruisers *Baleares* and *Canarias*. These aircraft were then used to form "He- 60 Squadron" in April 1937, which belonged to the Fleet, and were given the numbers 60-1, 60-2, 60-3, and 60-4.

Five of the Heinkel He 60s survived the war: two from the Nationalist Airforce (60-3 and 60-4) and three from the Condor Legion that bore the numbers 60-5, 60-6, and 60-7. The three Heinkel He 59s from the same formation were numbered 71-1, 71-2, and 71-3 from April 1939.

Finally, regarding the Heinkel He 59s of AS./88, it should be mentioned that they contiued to carry the un-hyphenated numbers throughout the war, and a few even operated without numbers at all, although in reports related to materiel they were referred to by their previously assigned official numbering. According to Sonderstab "W," a total of 27 Heinkel He 59s were received at a cost of 312,290 marks (RM) each.

1.3.- The first air operations and war service carried out by the seaplanes of AS./88 during the last quarter of 1936.

October

From their base at Puntales (Cadiz), the German Heinkel He 60s began patrolling and carrying out reconnaissance flights in support of the Nationalist Fleet; these took place between the Straits of Gibraltar to Almeria, and were effected under the command of *Hauptmann* Karl Heinz Wolf, first commander of AS./88 (from November 1936 to February 1937). As a reward for his efficient organization of the Squadron from its beginning, he was awarded the prestigious *Deutsche Spanien-Kreuz in Gold mit Schwertern und Brillanten*.

Heinkel He 60 number 512, named the "Sea Beast," following its emergency landing at sea near the Punta Almina lighthouse, in Ceuta.

The German destroyer "Luchs" was the ship which found the "Sea Beast" and towed it to the port of Melilla.

The first reference to a seaplane of the future Squadron appeared in a reconnaissance mission carried out on 6 October, when a Heinkel He 60, numbered 512 and with the name "Sea Beast" painted on its fuselage, had to make a forced landing 25 miles to the 090 of Almina point, resulting in the chief of the Nationalist Fleet authorizing the cruiser *Cervera* (radiogramme nº 185 dated 6 October) to put to sea, together with the gunboat *Cánovas del Castillo* and the patrol boats operating in the Straits, to go to its aid. The German battle cruiser *Admiral Scheer* and the destroyer *Luchs* also took part in the rescue, these latter ships locating the aircraft and towing it back to the port of Melilla.

The Heinkel 60s operating from Cádiz during the second fortnight of October reconnoitered the coast and also took part in attacks on the enemy air base at El Rompedizo (Málaga), from where the Goverment's Breguet XIXs and Vickers Vildebeest operated along the Malaga front. On 15 October two Heinkel He 60s bombed the aerodrome, causing extensive damage, and the Military Commander, Colonel Luis Romero Basart, heavily criticized the republican pilots for having allowed the attack to take place. It should be noted that in Málaga there were no fighters in service at that time, and on the following day (the 16th) the crew of a Breguet XIX, formed of Flight-Sargeant Ignacio Camarero and Bombardier Sargeant

German SC 10 (10 kg) bomb, identical to those dropped by the Condor Legion's Heinkel He 60s on the Republican aerodrome at El Rompedizo, in Malaga.

A crane in the port of Cadiz placing a Heinkel He 60 on chocks.

Benjamín Torres, had the determination to confront the Germans. These managed to bring down the enemy plane in flames, which resulted in the deaths of both its crew. This was the first aerial victory over an enemy plane by the future AS./88 Squadron.

Aerial view of El Rompedizo (Malaga), from where a Republican Breguet XIX took off to intercept two Heinkel He 60s and was shot down into the sea.

A Breguet XIX light bomber and reconnaissance aircraft like the one shot down over Malaga by two German seaplanes from what was to become Squadron AS./88.

November

On 6 November the German battle cruiser *Admiral Scheer* recovered a Heinkel He 60 from the sea that had suffered damage following a forced landing while flying along the Mediterranean coast. At the end of that month the Condor Legion was officially formed and the seaplanes were organized as the maritime reconnaissance squadron *Aufklärungsstaffel See /88* or AS./88, based at the port of Cádiz. On the 28th, the Heinkel He 60s numbered 512, 513, and 514 were operational.

Heinkel He 60 seaplane in flight.

The El Atalayon base in Melilla, where two Heinkel He 59s and four Heinkel He 60s of the recently created AS./88 were transferred for strategic reasons.

Heinkel He 59 of AS./88 with its original "Ace of Spades" emblem, until then relatively unknown. (Jesús López Morcillo collection, via Miguel Puchol)

December

The German cruiser *Königsberg* rescued a Heinkel He 59 which was in the sea and badly damaged on 19 December, taking it to port. It is doubtful this aircraft was returned to service.

On the 24th, the Commander in Chief of the Cadiz Maritime department sent a telegram to the Admiral appointed Chief of Staff of the Nationalist Navy, stating as follows: "*Possible arrival 'Baleares' on 28th. Request aircraft deployed to Jerez on 27th, reference my note of the 18th of this month. I inform you that aircraft 511, 512, 513, 514, 521, and 522 are to transfer to Melilla, leaving this Department without their services.*" The Nationalist cruiser *Baleares* arrived in Cadiz on 28 December 1936, and the previous mentioned aircraft were two twin-engined Heinkel He 59 seaplanes (521 and 522) and four single-engined Heinkel He 60s (511, 512, 513, and 514), which had to transfer their base from Puntales (Cádiz) to El Atalayón (Melilla) (see APPENDIX IV).

The presence of AS./88 in Melilla was to cause serious international tension, mainly with Great Britain and France, and the last mentioned country placed troops on the frontier with the Spanish protectorate in Morocco. However, in his New Year message for 1937 Adolf Hitler declared that Germany had no interest in either Spain nor Spanish territory in Morocco.

At the base in El Atalayón, a makeshift workshop was set up for torpedos. The torpedos themselves originated from the Horten (Norway) State Factory, and from 1934 were made under license by the firm Schwartzkopf in Kiel (Germany) and were designated the F5 air torpedo (*LT, Lufttorpedo*). However, these proved to be inferior in both performance and technical features to the Norwegian made torpedos.

German F 5 torpedo, a copy of the Norwegian Horten, which was used operationally for the first time during the Spanish Civil War. (J. M. Campesino collection, via Raúl Arias)

Above: Werner Klümper. Opposite: Frontal view of a Heinkel He 59 fitted with a Rheinmetall Lb 201 20 mm cannon.

2

The Main Area of Operations and War Service Involving the Seaplanes of AS./88 During the First Six Months of 1937

January

On 8 January the Heinkel He 60 numbered 514 and the Heinkel He 59 numbered 522 were undergoing repairs in Cadiz, while the rest of the German unit remained at the base in El Atalayón (Melilla), later taking part in the operations at Málaga.

14 January-14 Februaury 1937: The Malaga campaign

The Spanish mail ship *Delfín* (ex *Optic*), 1,253 tons, had been built in 1885 in the Harland & Wolf shipyard in Belfast (Northern Ireland). The vessel belonged to the Transmediterranean Company and acted as a mail carrier in the Republican zone. On 30 January 1937, it was spotted by the Heinkel He 59 of *Oberleutnant* Werner Klümper as it was steaming from Almería to Málaga carrying a cargo of flour for the Republican army. Klümper approached

The Spanish mail ship "Delfín" was first to fall victim to the bombs of AS./88.

the target, launched an F 5 air torpedo, and turned. But the torpedo failed to drop due to an electrical fault. After two attempts, on the third his mechanic managed to free it, although the torpedo fell in a circular motion and failed to hit the target. This was to be the first torpedo to be dropped since the end of the First World War. Klümper went back to El Atalayon and returned some hours later, this time carrying four 250 kg bombs and accompanied by two other aircraft. The *Delfín* was attacked again, and this time received two hits when it had run aground at Calaceite beach (Malaga), and the ship was lost. Their had been an enemy defense consisting of fighters. Other sources insist that the *Delfín* had been torpedoed prior to the seaplane attack by the Italian submarine *Ciro Menotti* (Captain Vittorio Moccagatta, Silver bar to the Military Valour Medal) and had been finished off by the seaplane. Klümper was to go on to command the *Luftwaffe's* KG 26 torpedo plane squadron during World War II.

The report of the Republican Air and Naval Ministry dated 2 February describes the attack as follows: "*Three enemy torpedo planes bombed the merchant ship 'Delfín' which had run aground on Calaceite beach. Once our Air Force received the alert, four fighters were scrambled, which then engaged the enemy aircraft, forcing them to flee.*"

February

It was at this time that there was a change of command at the German squadron. *Hauptmann* Karl Heinz Wolf returned to Berlin and was relieved by *Hauptmann* Günther Klünder, who would later become second in command of the AS./88 (February to July 1937).

The Spanish steamer *Nuria Ramos* (ex *María Elisa*, ex *Rufina*, ex *Algorteño*, ex *Roumania*), of 2,733 tons, had been built in 1893 by William Gray & Co. Ltd in West Hartlepool (England). The ship belonged to Hijos de Ramón and A. Ramos of Barcelona.

The vessel made two voyages from Barcelona to Orán, returning to Barcelona loaded with coal. On a third, similar voyage, as it was returning from Orán, under command of Captain Estrader, adherent to the Republican cause, carrying two hundred foreign volunteers on board, it was intercepted by a Heinkel He 59 of AS./88 on 31 January 1937, as it was underway near Cabo de Palos. This aircraft, commanded by *Oberleutnant* Werner Klümper, had taken off from El Atalayón carrying an F 5 torpedo, accompanied by the Heinkel He 60 of *Leutnant* Dieter Leicht. After firing warning shots, the seaplanes forced the merchantman to turn about and enter the port of Melilla. From there it was given a new crew and taken first to Ceuta and later Cádiz, where it remained.

The Republican newspaper ABC reported the incident on 20 Februaury 1937, under the headline "*Ship detained by Rebels*" and continued: "*Today, news has been received that the Spanish ship Nuria Ramos left Oran on 30 January on a course for Alicante, carrying 103 Spanish nationals.On the 31st at eleven O'clock in the morning, some 40 miles from Cabo de Palos, two rebel aircraft approached the ship, forcing it to enter the port of Melilla, where it arrived during the early hours of the 1st of this month. All the crew and passengers were detained in Melilla.*"

Elsewhere, the AS./88 took part with all its available aircraft in the capture of Málaga. On 5 February, one of the Heinkel He 59s taking part in the operation (number 523) crashed into the sea following a dogfight with Republican Polikarpov I-15 "Chato" fighters flying from the El Rompedizo (Málaga) aerodrome, flown by Russian, American, and Spanish pilots. The republican pilots claimed two of the seaplanes shot down. One Heinkel He 59 (523) was severely damaged, and what remained of the aircraft was sunk by the 20 and 40 mm cannon on board the Nationalist cruiser *Canarias*. The plane's observer, *Leutnant*

Twin-engined Heinkel He 59 of AS./88. The first of these planes was lost following a dog fight on 5 Ovctober 1937, off the coast of Malaga.

Above: The Nationalist cruiser "Canarias" off Malaga in February 1937. Observe the forward 203.2/50 mm guns. With an angle of elevation of 70 degrees the guns could be used in the anti-aircraft role. Below: Heinkel 60 (512) "Sea Beast" aboard the cruiser "Canarias."

Dieter Leicht, died soon after from his wounds, while his comrades held him onto the floating remains of the aircraft. Another of the seaplanes, a Heinkel He 60 (512) bearing the name "Sea Beast" on its fuselage sides, was damaged, with part of the upper surface of its left wing broken, its propeller split and pilot wounded. The *Canarias* rescued the four crew members from each plane and the body of the deceased German airman. This was AS./88's first combat death.

The "Sea Beast" is winched aboard the "Canarias."

The Republican Air and Naval Ministry report of 5 February 1937 recounted events as follows: "*On the Malaga front, our fighters were constantly engaged with enemy aircraft, managing to shoot down a seaplane which crashed into the sea*."

Ten days later, AS./88 was transferred from El Atalayón (Melilla) to a temporary base at the port of Málaga, from where the Heinkel He 59s and Heinkel 60s began operations.

March

On 18 March a new version of the Heinkel He 60 entered service with AS./88, designated 515, based initially in Cádiz. The following day the aircraft took off at 0900 h heading for Málaga, arriving at 1020 h. As it was landing the aircraft flipped over, although the crew were unhurt. The aircraft was recovered but spent a long time undergoing repairs.

Five days later, on the 23rd, a Heinkel He 59 (525) left Malaga at 1230 h on reconnaissance, returning at 1630 h. The crew reported that fifteen miles north of the Island of Alboran they had seen a French ship, the *Aden*, heading to the east coast of Spain, making ten knots and carrying aboard the typical camouflaged crates used for transporting aircraft.

On 24 March a new Heinkel He 59 (526) left Cádiz and landed in Málaga, which meant there were then all four of the Heinkel He 59 numbered 522, 524, 525, and 526, as well as the Heinkel He 60 (513) in flight and the other (515) undergoing repairs.

April

On 9 April three twin-engined Tupoliev SB "Katiuskas" of the Republican nº 12 Group bombed AS./88's temporary base, which had been set up in Malaga since the previous month, killing *Gefreiter* Siegfried Papendieck. A telegram sent by the Civil Governor of Malaga described the attack as follows: "*At 0900 today three red aircraft approached the base at Hidros dropping six bombs killing eight and leaving another eight wounded, although the base itself was undamaged*."

The following day the Heinkel He 59s numbered 522 and 524 were transferred to Cadiz, landing at 0715 h. On the 12th aircraft numbers 525 and 526 did the same, while the Heinkel He 60 number 513 remained in Malaga. This last mentioned aircraft transferred to Cadiz on the 18th, leaving the Hidros base in Malaga empty.

20 April 1937: Control by the non-intervention naval committeeenters into effect.

The next day, a Heinkel He 60 (513) marked "Sea Wolf" had an accident while landing at the port of Huelva, which was described in the report of the Commander in Chief of the Southern Army as follows: "*The Military Governor of Huelva has reported that at eleven o'clock yesterday, 21st, the seaplane number 513 crashed while taking off. The aircraft was being flown by Major Rosi, commander of the Italian naval base and a German called Mahi, both of whom were injured. The aircraft is inoperative*." The seaplane had to be sent to Cadiz for repairs.

The Republican twin-engined Tupoliev SB "Katiuskas" bombed AS./88 seaplanes in the port of Malaga, resulting in one death.

Aerial view of the port of Malaga, the provisional base for AS./88.

Heinkel 60 (513) "Sea Wolf" spent several months undergoing repairs following an accident that occurred during landing in the port of Huelva.

Since the beginning of that year, whenever the location of the Republican Fleet became known, AS./88 sent up one or two seaplanes in order to attack it with torpedos. On 25 April a Heinkel He 59, acting on information transmitted by the German cruiser *Leipzig*, which was shadowing the Republican Fleet, launched an F 5 torpedo attack near Motril (Granada) without hitting the target.

That same day, the three engine Junkers Ju 52/3m (W) numbered 527 joined the squadron in Cadiz and carried out a reconnaissance mission.

May

At five o'clock in the afternoon on 6 May, the cruiser *Leipzig* encountered the Republican cruisers *Libertad* and *Méndez Núñez*, along with five destroyers at sea, as they were leaving the port of Cartagena to escort the *Ciudad de Cádiz*, which was returning from the U.S.S.R, advising the three Heinkel He 59s of AS./88 present in the area of their location. One of the aircraft dropped a torpedo which passed close to the stern of the *Libertad*, while the bombs dropped on the enemy ships missed their targets.

The Nationalist Air Force operational order nº 385, dated 10 May, had as its objective the forcing of the old Republican battleship *Jaime I* from the port of Almería in an attempt to sink her. According to that order, five Heinkel He 59s armed with F 5 torpedos crewed by German airmen based in Malaga would participate in the operation.

Following a meeting aboard the German cruiser *Nürnberg* on 14 May 1937 in the waters near Cadiz, the Nationalist commanders asked the Germans and Italians to intensify their air attacks against the *Jaime I*, the only Republican warship capable of defeating their

The Republican battleship "Jaime I." With its powerful 305 mm guns it was the only Republican vessel that could threaten the Nationalist fleet.

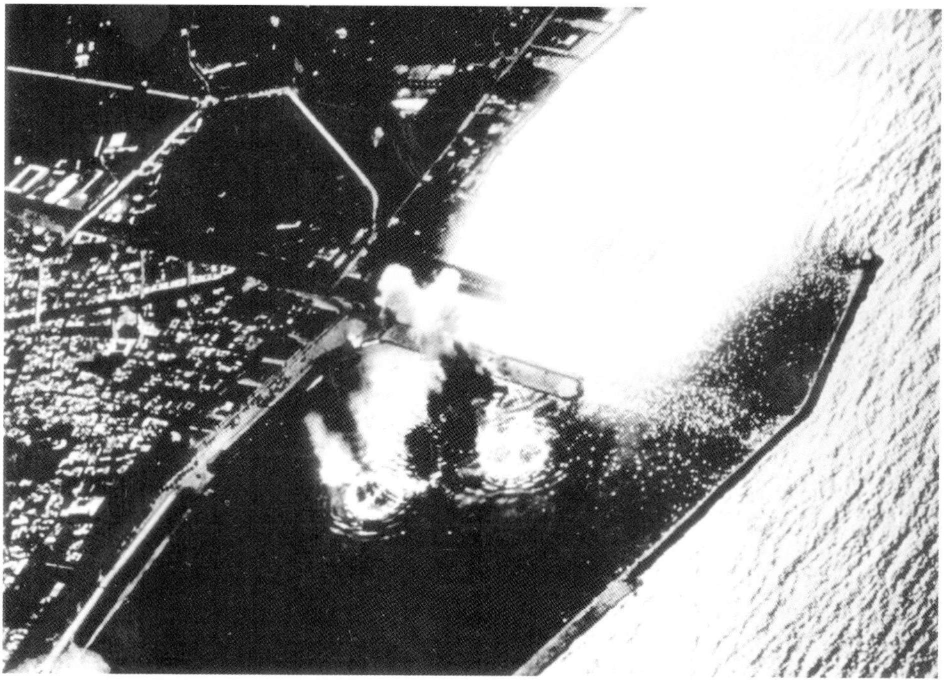

The "Jaime I" was bombed while it lay in the port of Almeria in an attempt to force it out to sea, where it could be torpedoed by five Heinkel He 59s operating from Malaga.

cruisers with its powerful 12 inch guns. It was agreed that the air attacks would be made by both the Italian aircraft operating from the Balearic Islands and the seaplanes of AS./88.

On 19 May 1937 at 0500 hours, a Heinkel He 59 (524) took off and later landed at Cadiz at 1000 hours. The objective of the aircraft's reconnaissance patrol was to confirm that the *Jaime I* continued to remain moored in Almeria.

The attacks on the *Jaime I* began on 21 May 1937, and a 100 kg bomb dropped by a Savoia Marchetti S.M. 79 perforated the ships armour, causing slight damage and wounding twenty of its crew.

Three days later, in the early hours of the morning, the Heinkel He 59 piloted by *Leutnant zur See* Albert Calmberg dropped a 250 kg with no effect.

29 May 1937: Republican aircraft bomb the German battle cruiser Deutschland.

June

The official information bulletin of the general staff of the Cádiz area Maritime department, dated 9 June 1937, recorded the dropping of another F 5 torpedo; this time the target was a Republican destroyer, and the report states that:

"*At 19:25 h a 'Negrillo' (German) seaplane took off on a reconnaissance flight, spotting the 'Almirante Antequera' 50 miles west of Larach and heading for there. On observing the plane the 'red' destroyer began to zig-zag. At 21:35 the seaplane dropped a torpedo which missed by a small margin. The 'Antequera' answered with anti-aircraft fire steering 300° for some 25 miles. The aircraft returned at 22:50 h, without incident.*"

On 25 June, in telegram n° 5.957 sent at 1905 h, General Hugo Sperrle, commander of the Condor Legion, adressed the Commander in Chief of the Nationalist Air Force, General Alfredo Kindelán, asking him: "*Are you still thinking of transferring the seaplane reconnaissance squadron, which is going to be augmented by a further six aircraft, to Palma? Please answer by teletypewriter.*" To which General Kindelán answered at 21.00 h saying "*In effect I am very interested in concentrating your seaplanes on the Island of Mallorca, and am pleased to hear they will be increased by six.*"

Elsewhere, on 28 June, a dogfight took place northeast of Cabo de Palos (Cartagena) between two seaplanes: a Heinkel He 59 of AS./88 and a Republican Dornier *Wal*. According to the testimony of the Dornier crewman Corporal Machinegunner-Bombardier Francisco Caballero Sandoval, the combat developed as follows: "*...while carrying out a reconnaissance flight northeast of Cabo de Palos, we engaged a twin-engined Heinkel, and*

The Dornier Wal D-2 from the Republican Naval Air Service that was shot down by Heinkel He 59 number 522 off Cabo de Palos.

were shot down. As a result of this action I temporarily lost the use of my right hand, for which I was recommended for the 'Sufrimientos por la Patria' (wounded in the service of the homeland) Medal, and promoted to Sargeant, after passing an exam, on 3 September that same year."

The shot down aircraft was a Republican Dornier *Wal*, which had belonged to the Naval Air Service and was crewed by the pilot, Lieutenant Jaime Fernández Villalba, the radio operator, Lieutenant Gonzalo Rodríguez Hernández, Flight Enginieer and Bombardier Lieutenant Luis Sarabia Hurtado, who was killed, and the previously mentioned Francisco Caballero, who was wounded on the right hand. The Dornier was forced to make an emergency landing in the sea and the Heinkel He 59 made several passes, machine-gunning the plane until it caught fire. The action was witnessed by the British steamship *Nailsea Manor*, which found the downed aircraft nineteen miles at 47° from Cabo de Palos. The ship rescued the crew and took them to Cartagena.

According to Francisco Caballero's flight record, the Dornier *Wal* was n° 2 and had taken off from Los Alcázares air base on a reconnaissance flight at 10:40 h that morning, and was attacked by the Heinkel He 59 twenty-three miles northeast of Cabo de Palos.

The report by the Cadiz Maritime described the Heinkel He 59 as being number 522, and that during its return from Palma to Cadiz it had engaged an enemy Dornier enemy, which it had destroyed.

Aerial view of the seaplane base at Los Alcazares, from where the Dornier Wal had taken off.

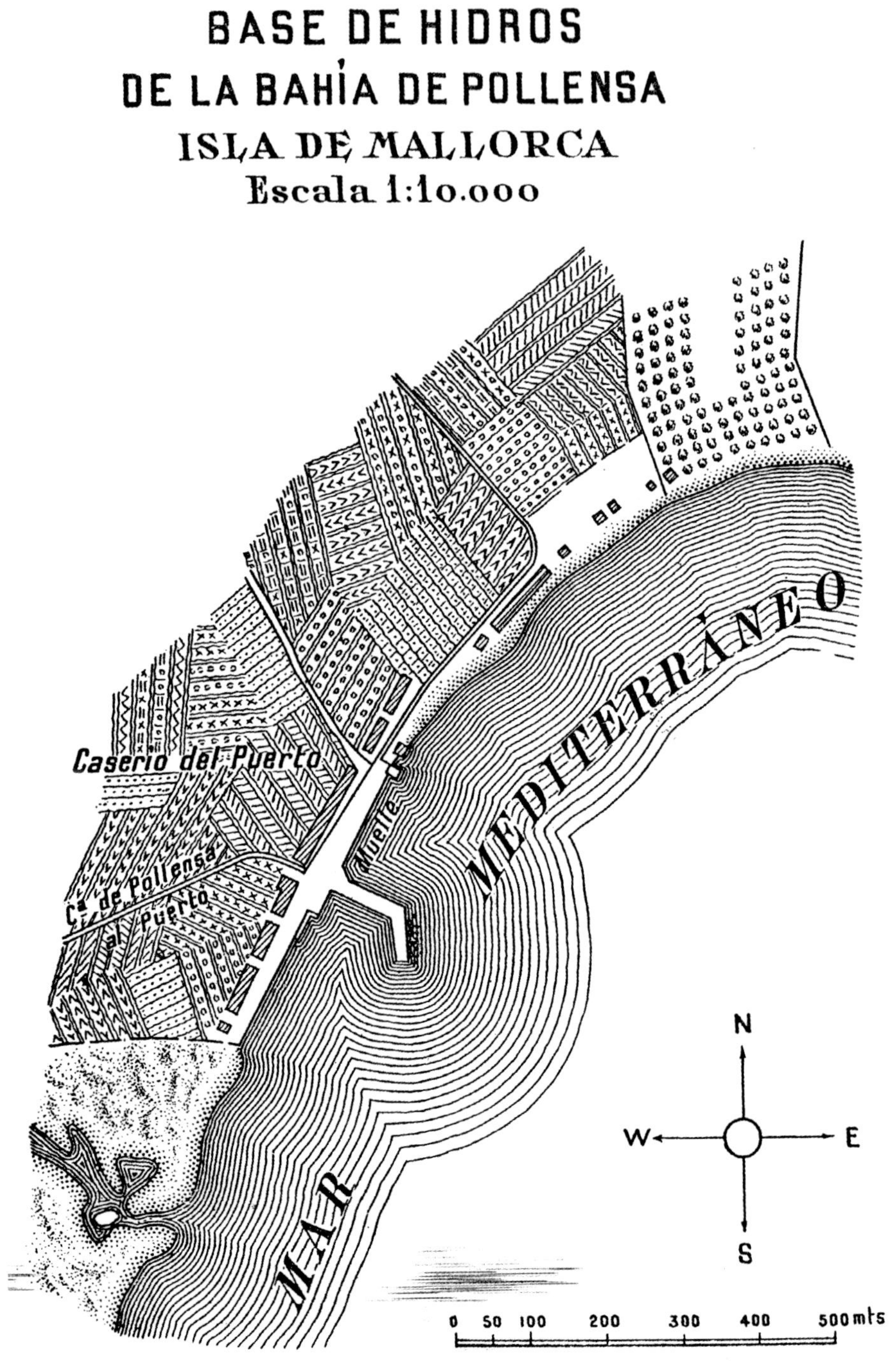
BASE DE HIDROS
DE LA BAHÍA DE POLLENSA
ISLA DE MALLORCA
Escala 1:10.000
Caserio del Puerto
Cª de Pollensa al Puerto
Muelle
MAR MEDITERRÁNEO
N
W
E
S
0 50 100 200 300 400 500 mts

3

Transfer to the Balearic Islands

After being successively based in Puntales (Cadiz), El Atalayon (Melilla), puerto de Malaga port, and again in Puntales (Cadiz), AS./88 was transferred to the Balearic Islands, at Pollensa (Mallorca), which became its permanent base until the end of the conflict.

The main part of the transfer occurred between 15 and 25 July 1937. Two Heinkel He 59 flew to the island on 15 July and the other two remained in Cadiz, awaiting spare parts. The Junkers Ju 52/3m (W), with the advanced Headquarters, had been in Pollensa since 9 July. Three new Heinkel He 59s had arrived by air on 6 July. The Squadron's personnel and equipment were sent to Palma aboard a steamship. At first the installations in Pollensa were improvised and set up at speed, so that operations could begin as soon as possible. The hotels "Illa d´Or," "Marimar," and "Mar y Cielo," which were near the base, were requisitioned, as were some private houses, in order to accommodate all the Squadron's personnel and

Jetty at the base at Pollensa, where several Heinkel He 59s can be seen at anchor.

additional troops who were later to reach 110 men. Later, permanent accommodation was built inside the Pollensa base. Initially there were five Heinkel He 59s and a Junkers Ju 52/3 m operation. At the beginning of August, once the spare parts had arrived, there were seven Heinkel He 59s available to fly. All of AS./88 was considered, in terms of maintenance and accommodation, the guests of the Nationalist Air Force.

In the Balearic Islands at this time, the Nationalist Air Force disposed of a De Havilland D.H. 60 "Moth" numbered 30-7 (ex civil EC-AFI), which had remained at the flying school at the Son Bonet aerodrome.

At times Pollensa hosted a flight of Nationalist Dornier Wals, as well as the Cant Z-501s of Group 2 G-62, which were based there permanently.

In regards seaplanes, the Nationalist Air Force in the Isalands, under Lieutenant Colonel Ramón Franco, had five Cant Z-501s and a Savoia S-62, integrated in G-62 Group 2, stationed at Pollensa. Furthermore, they could occasionally count on a flight of Dornier *Wals* located at Alcudia bay.

The Italian Legion's air component, under Colonel Aprile, was more numerous. They had a fighter Group at Son San Juan aerodrome equipped with nine Fiat CR.32 "Chirris" and a night bomber Group with nine Savoia Marchetti SM.81s. The Italians also had an aircraft park with workshops and repair facilities at Son Bonet aerodrome. Their three Macchi M.41 seaplanes were initially based at Palma de Mallorca, but were later moved to Alcudia, where they were tasked with patrolling and maritime surveillance.

With regard to the "Negrilla" (the official codename for the Condor Legion's air component), AS./88 at first had only seven Heinkel He 59s, tasked with bombing and torpedo missions, as well as a Junkers Ju 52/3m (W) fitted with floats for transport and reconnaissance, all of them based at Pollensa. Sporadically, they also had one or two Heinkel He 60s at their disposal.

As an anecdote, it is worth mentioning that some members of AS./88 were naval pilots from the *Kriegsmarine*, who stood out for their important work as operations chiefs at the German Naval Mission in Palma de Mallorca. Among them were *Korvetten Kapitän* Georg Johannes Strauch (January to October 1938) and *Kapitän-Leutnant* Karl Knappe (January to April 1939), as well as the pilots and observers Auffermann, Bigalk, Bammer, Calmberg, Deecke, Dieterischs, Fiehn, Fritsch, Hochbaum, Hörstke, Jandrey, Keese, Kettner, Lohmeyer, Metzger, Poeschel, Reefe, Schneider, Thomsen, Toball, and Wodtke.

Only three Spanish Heinkel He 60s (60-1, 60-2, and 60-4) remained in Melilla from "Escuadrilla He-60" (He-60 squadron), while a fourth (60-3) was being repaired at the La Carraca arsenal (Cadiz)

Boat used to supply fuel to the seaplanes at the base. In the background is one of the Macchi M.41s from the base at Alcudia.

4

The Blockade of the Mediterranean

It would be impossible to speak of the blockade of the Republican ports along the Mediterranean coast during the Spanish Civil War without making reference to the island that made it all possible: Mallorca.

The island was in Nationalist hands from the beginning of the war, and was in a crucial geo-strategic location for controlling shipping in the western Mediterranean; at the same time, it made for a giant unsinkable aircraft carrier facing the coasts of Catalonia and southeastern Spain.

It was in the middle of July 1937, in Salamanca, when the strategic thinking behind the aero-naval blockade of the Mediterranean was given shape in operational order number 318, issued from the Generalisimo's General Staff and signed by Francisco Franco himself on the 15th of that month.

By virtue of this order, the seven Heinkel He 59s, which on this date were flying to Pollensa, together with the Nationalist and Italian aircraft stationed on the island, had as their main objective:

"*to intensify the agressive action from the air against the enemy fleet, his communications*

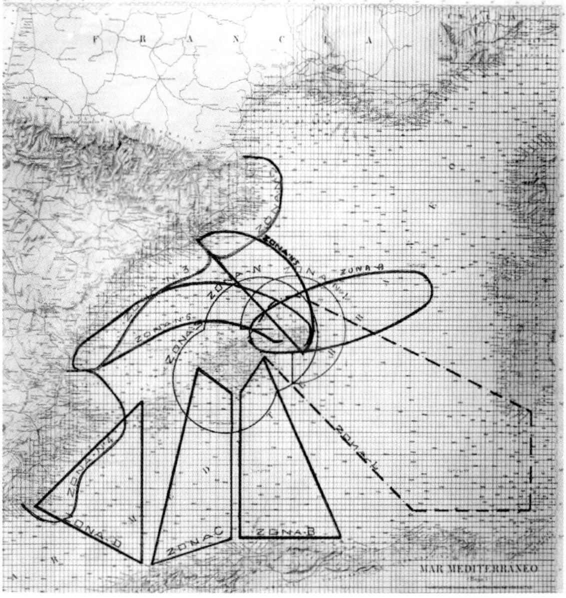

Page 36: A visit to the Pollensa base by a group of local Naval Falangists.

Left: Map of the Mediterranean distributed by the staff of the Balearic Naval Command showing the different areas of surveillance pertaining to the International Non-intervention Committee.

Visit by Admiral Moreno, Commander in Chief of the Mediterranean blockade, to the aerodrome at Son San Juan de Mallorca. On the right is Lieutenant Colonel Ramon Franco, Balearic Air Region commander.

and ports, and in this way collaborating with the naval blockade of the Mediterranean conducted by our fleet."

The seven seaplanes of AS./88 were to operate in close liaison with the naval command on the island, and its main missions were to be:

a) Observe the enemy fleet.
b) Agressive action against the same both at sea and in port.
c) Bombing missions against coastal military targets.
d) Attack Republican shipping in the territorial waters and any ship attempting to break the blockade.

Frontal view of a Heinkel He 59 of AS./88.

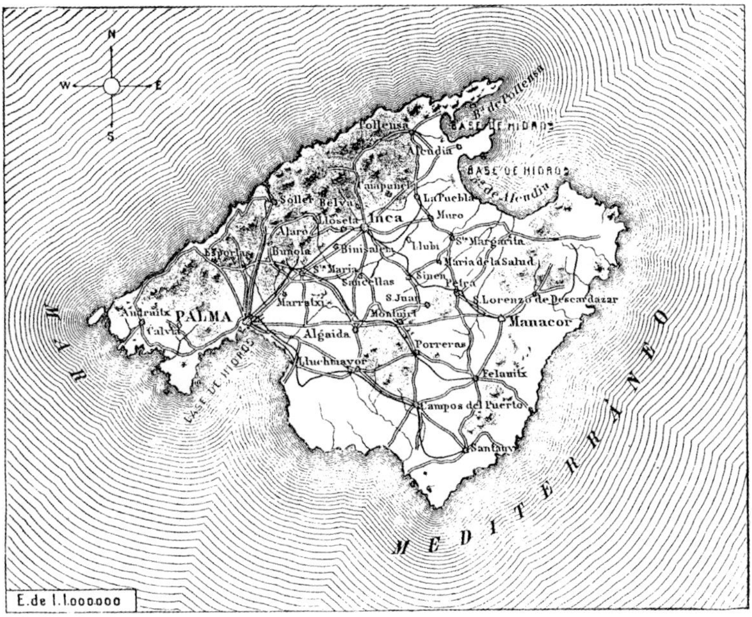

Map of Mallorca.

e) Advise Palma and the fleet on the location and route of enemy ships or those attempting to run the blockade in the case that these aircraft execute the mission.
f) Some assistance would come in the form of armed speed boats.

To coordinate air operations and liaise with the Navy, a regional general staff was set up under command of the commander of Air Forces in Mallorca (Lieutenant Colonel Ramon Franco) with representatives from the different units involved.

Later, on 3 August, the Commander in Chief of the Nationalist Air Force, General Kindelan, issued the commander of Air Forces in Mallorca (Lieutenant Colonel Ramon Franco) with a complementary order to Operational Order 318, which established the following:

"*The admiral in charge of the Mallorca naval base is to have a naval pilot as a technical advisor and liaison between the different air units stationed on the island, while circumstances dictate that it continues to be unadvisable to establish a General Staff for the blockade on Mallorca*."

Ramon Franco and the Italian Colonel Mario Bernasconi in the cathedral in Palma de Mallorca.

5

The Blockade from July to December 1937. Main Air Operations and War Service of AS./88

July

At this time AS./88 received another commander. *Hauptmann* Günther Klünder returned to Germany and was relieved by *Hauptmann* Hans Hefele, who became the third commander of AS./88 (July 1937 to January 1938).

Inmediately, the Heinkel He 59s returned to their war service in the new theatre of operations, carrying out long reconnaissance missions along Spain's eastern coast, and on many occasions being subjected to anti-aircraft fire and often the attentions of the

One of the Heinkel He 59s fitted with the Rheinmetall Lb. 201 20 mm cannon for defense against Republican fighters.

The merchant ship "Chepo" was attacked by three Heinkel He 59s from AS./88, which killed four of its crew and caused serious damage to the stern, forcing the vessel to run aground near Calella.

Republican night-fighters, who they managed to keep at a distance with the saeplanes' weapons—especially the Rheinmetall Lb. 201 20 mm cannon—or by dropping down to sea level.

The Republican destroyers *Almirante Antequera*, *Churruca*, *Escaño*, and *Gravina* left the port of Cartagena at dusk on 19 July, joining the destroyers *Almirante Valdés* and *Almirante Miranda* fourteen miles from Valencia at dawn the next day. A squadron of

Republican torpedo boats numbers 31 and 41 in a French port. Number 41 was sunk by the German seaplanes as it escorted the "Chepo."

Italian planes spotted the six destroyers and informed Palma. Immediately a patrol of three Heinkel He 59s took off, armed with F5 torpedos. Following a reconnaissance in which they were unable to find the enemy vessels, the operation was cancelled.

On 30 July a patrol of three Heinkel He 59s spotted a Republican convoy outbound from Marsailles, some fifteen miles from Arenys de Mar. The convoy was made up of the Greek merchant ship *Laris* camouflaged as the Panamanian vessel *Chepo*, and carrying a consignment of arms. Escorting it were the Republican destroyers *Almirante Valdés* and *Escaño*, along with two torpedo boats (numbers 31 and 41, Russian built Type G-5s). According to the official report of AS./88, in the ensuing attack the merchant ship was hit in the stern, the destroyer *Almirante Valdés* suffered damage to its prow, and torpedo boat number 41 was destroyed. Added to this, an enemy Breguet XIX was shot down, although its crew escaped unhurt. There were four men killed aboard the *Chepo* and the ship ran aground near Calella. At the same time, one of the attacking Heinkel He 59s was hit and was obliged to make a forced landing about fifteen miles south of Blanes with wounded on board. The Nationalist cruiser *Canarias* came to its assistance and observed that the 5 knot southeasterly wind was pushing it towards the enemy coast. The cruiser stopped engines and sent a launch to rescue the crew, among them the then commander of AS./88, *Hauptmann/Flieger* Hans Hefele. The seaplane was taken in tow and arrived in Pollensa at 08:00 hours the next day.

August

On the night of 3/4 August a patrol of three Heinkel He 59s bombed the port of Barcelona, dropping six 250 kg bombs with large explosions beeing seen in the commercial area of the docks. The seaplanes were intercepted by Republican night-fighters, which left a German airman with a wounded thigh.

The AS./88 report for the 6th states that: "*On 4.8.37 a flight of seaplanes bombed a ship aground near Calella, with six 250 kg bombs, with one of the bombs hitting the target*." This was the previously mentioned *Laris* (*Chepo*).

On 12 August the Danish refrigerator ship *Edith* (1,566 tons), built in the Nakskov Skibs shipyard (Denmark) and belonging to J. Lauritzen of Copenhague, was

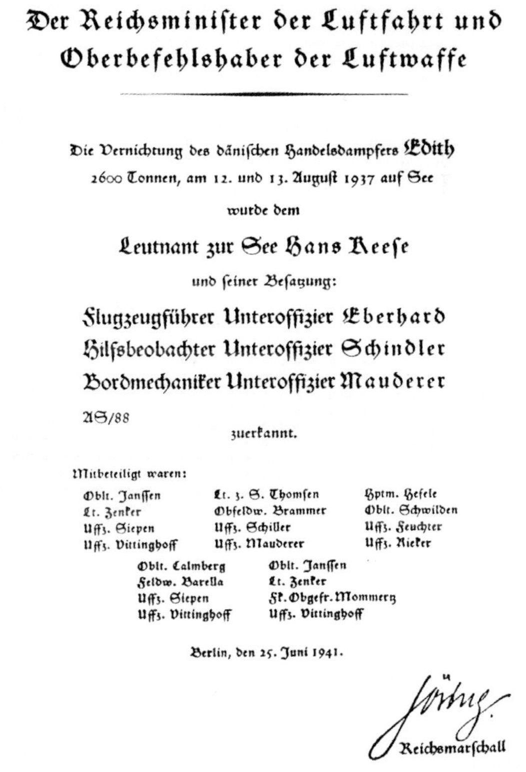

Der Reichsminister der Luftfahrt und Oberbefehlshaber der Luftwaffe

Die Vernichtung des dänischen Handelsdampfers **Edith**
2600 Tonnen, am 12. und 13. August 1937 auf See
wurde dem

Leutnant zur See Hans Reese

und seiner Besatzung:

Flugzeugführer Unteroffizier Eberhard
Hilfsbeobachter Unteroffizier Schindler
Bordmechaniker Unteroffizier Mauderer

AS/88

zuerkannt.

Mitbeteiligt waren:

Oblt. Janssen	Lt. z. S. Thomsen	Hptm. Hefele
Lt. Zenker	Obfeldw. Brammer	Oblt. Schwilden
Uffz. Siepen	Uffz. Schiller	Uffz. Feuchter
Uffz. Vittinghoff	Uffz. Mauderer	Uffz. Rieker
Oblt. Calmberg	Oblt. Janssen	
Feldw. Barella	Lt. Zenker	
Uffz. Siepen	Fk. Obgefr. Mommerz	
Uffz. Vittinghoff	Uffz. Vittinghoff	

Berlin, den 25. Juni 1941.

Göring
Reichsmarschall

Heinkel He 59s numbers 528 and 529 were responsible for the bombing of the British ship "Noemijulia" as it sailed near Barcelona, forcing her to seek refuge in Port Vendrés.

attacked in the afternoon with 50 and 250 kg bombs by a patrol of four Heinkel He 59s from AS./88 forty miles from Tortosa while it was transporting a cargo of frozen meat from Marsailles to Valencia. The ship caught fire and was left adrift until it was torpedoed and sunk the next day by another Heinkel He 59. The crew of twenty men, one of whom was wounded, managed to save themselves with the ship's life boats, as well as the French officer on board representing the Committee for non-intervention. The survivors were picked up by fishing boats and taken to shore. The wounded man died a few days later.

Officially the sinking was attributed to the Heinkel He 59 of *Leutnant zur See* Hans Reefe. His crew was formed of *Unteroffizier* (pilot) Peter Eberhard, *Unteroffizier / Beobachter* Heinrich Schindler, and *Unteroffizier /Bordmechaniker* Mauderer.

The attack was described in the AS./88 report dated 13 August: "*Seaplanes.- on the afternoon of 12.08.37, a flight bombed the Danish flagged vessel 'Edith' on the wishes of the Spanish Admiral, dropping fifteen 50 k. and two 250 kg bombs, which fell on and around the ship, setting it on fire which caused the crew to abandon ship.*"

According to the (Secret) report dated 2 October 1937, prior to the bombing of the *Edith* one of the Heinkel He 59s dropped a F 5 torpedo, which missed. The following day, when the ship was adrift, on fire, and leaning, it was torpedoed by another Heinkel He 59, which succeeded in sinking it.

Elsewhere, on 23 August the British ship *Noemijulia* (ex *Noemí*, ex *Barlby*), 2,499 tons, built in 1895 by Ropner & Son, Stockton (England), and belonging to Noemijulia S.S. Co. Ltd., was bombed as it was underway near Barcelona by two Heinkel He 59s of AS./88, which had the numbers 528 and 529 on their fuselages, and was finally able to seek shelter in Port Vendres.

The Republican ABC newspaper, in a hurried report, described the agression as follows: "*S.O.S. from an English ship bombed by two rebel aircraft.- The Marsailles radio-telegraph office intercepted the following message, sent by the British ship Noemijulia after being attacked by two rebel aircraft: 'We are being bombed. Our position is 42° 7´ North and 5° 32´ East. The attacking aircraft bear the numbers 528 and 529, a black circle with a white cross and two black bars.*"

Two Republican aircraft answered the call for help and attacked the seaplanes without results. It can be seen that two new Heinkel He 59s had been incorporated into the AS./88 with the numbers 528 and 529.

The AS./88 report for 25 August also records the shooting down of a Republican fighter by a Heinkel He 59:

"*AS./88. Seaplane flight.- On 24.8, while bombing two ships unloading their cargo at Rosas, were attacked by two 'red' fighters. One of the enemy fighters was hit in the engine and was shot down.*" It seems the plane could have been a Polikarpov I-15 "Chato," although there is no official confirmation.

The port of Rosas was bombed several times by Heinkel He 59s of AS./ 88, as it was the port used for unloading Russian war materiel arriving from Marsailles.

September

On 4 September two Heinkel He 59s dropped eight 250 kg bombs from an altitude of 300 metres on the C.A.M.P.S.A. installations at Tarragona, hitting three of the fuel tanks, which burned for five days. Fire fighters were called in from Reus and Barcelona to help extinguish the fire. One of the tanks contained alcohol, producing high reaching blue flames that spectacularly lit up the city at night. In spite of the serious damage inflicted on the installations there was no loss of life or injuries. The consequences of this attack were important for the Republic, causing great difficulties for the offensive being conducted at that time on the Aragon front, which was attempting to divert Nationalist efforts from Asturias. Even the Republic's president, Manuel Azaña, in his daily meeting with the head of the government, recognized the importance of this bombing raid, stating: "*The enemy's aircraft have set light to the fuel tanks at Tarragona, which will no doubt create difficulties for the offensive*."

The following day AS./88 entered its official report recording the events:

"*AS/88 (Palma de Mallorca seaplane flight). On 4.9 carried out a bombing raid on the rail head at Tarragona which has been destroyed. At the same time, the CAMPSA fuel tanks on the western outskirts of Tarragona were also set on fire. Explosions and a large fire were seen. Enemy anti-aircraft batteries opened fire on the attacking aircraft*."

September 7th saw the incident known as the Cape Cherchel fight between the Nationalist cruiser *Baleares* and part of the Republican squadron, composed of two cruisers

Both the port of Tarragona and the CAMPSA installations, located in the outskirts of the city, were priority targets for AS./ 88 throughout the war.

The Nationalist cruiser "Baleares," which received the support of four Heinkel He 59s from AS./ 88, one of which was carrying an F 5 torpedo, during the engagement at Cabo Cherchel.

and eight destroyers. Four Heinkel He 59s of AS./88, one of which was armed with an F5 torpedo, took off from Pollensa at 13:30 hours. The torpedo was dropped but missed its target. The aircraft dropped their bombs around the Republican cruiser *Méndez Núñez* and the destroyers *Jorge Juan* and *Lepanto*, covering the ships in enourmous columns of water and smoke, and it appeared as though they had been hit, but this was not the case, and their unmistakable silhouettes soon reappeared.

Six days later, on the evening of the 13th, a patrol of Heinkel He 59s bombed the strategic railway bridge at Culera (Gerona), destroying it.

On 14 September at 06:30 hours, a flight of Heinkel He 59s attacked the Republican coastguard vessel *V-15 Llobregat* near Mataro. The ship was in the process of escorting the *Cabo Tres Forcas* from the frontier to Barcelona. The attack left one man killed and three men wounded, as well as causing damage to the ship. Later on, one of the Heinkels machine-gunned and damaged an Air France mail plane, which was running the service Marsailles to Barcelona.

Two days later, on the 16th, a patrol of three Heinkel He 59s bombed the train station at Port Bou. Two of the Heinkels were attacked by a French monoplane fighter that had come from the French frontier, but was forced to retire in the face of the 20 mm cannon fire. Next, the aircraft were attacked by four Spanish fighters, which were also beaten off and forced to withdraw towards France. The German pilots later declared to their commander on their honor that they had not crossed into French territory, "*not one inch*."

The Spanish cargo ship *Guecho* (ex *Canadian Trapper*), 3,276 tons, was built in 1920 by Davie S.B. Repairing Co., Levis P.Q. (Canada), and was the property of Amaya S.A.

The Spanish freighter "Guecho," sunk at Valencia by AS./ 88.

of Bilbao, a company that from the beginning of the war participated with its entire fleet in favor of the Republic. The *Guecho*, which was operating at the end of 1936 under the name *Guenecho*, was at Feodosia, loading war material, in August 1937. From there it weighed anchor and headed for Valencia, where it dropped anchor at the beginning of September. On the 14th it was making ready to continue its voyage to Barcelona, escorted by a flotilla of Republican destroyers. However, as the *Guecho* was leaving its propellor touched one of the chains on the destroyer *Escaño*, causing both ships to have to delay their departure. In the early hours of 16 September the *Guecho* was bombed and sunk by a flight of Italian Savoia Marchetti S.M. 81 night bombers in the port of Valencia. The attack by the

The Republican destroyer "Escaño."

Italians also damaged the destroyer *Escaño* and a British merchant ship, the *Jean Weems*. Nevertheless, it was not until sixteen days later that the ship sank completely after being finished off by Heinkel He 59s of AS./88. The *Guecho* was refloated on 23 May 1940 and was again put into service.

17 September 1937: Signing of the Nyon Agreement

On 24 September, the head of the Nationalist Air Force, General Kindelan, sent the commander of the Condor Legion the following telegram:

"*I sincerely regret the accidents involving the meteorological aircraft on the 21st and the Heinkel He 111 on the 23rd and I would like to take this opportunity to congratualate the Legion and the seaplanes in the Balearic Islands for their service*."

On 29 September several Heinkel He 59s of AS./88 bombed the bacteria laboratories (sic) near Barcelona, with the bombs falling close to the laboratories and factory. The official report was probably referring to one of the chemical factories in Flix or Badalona.

On an indetermined date during this month, a Heinkel He 59 of AS./88 commanded by *Leutnant zur See* Ernst Thomsen was attacked by a Republican Polikarpov I-16 "Mosca" fighter, receiving hits in both engines, and was forced to make an emergency landing at sea between Barcelona and Pollensa.

Republican Polikarpov I-16 "Mosca" fighter. It was one of these planes that attacked the Heinkel He 59 commanded by Thomsen, causing damage to the engines.

October

AS./88 also carried out some missions on its own initiative, and at times involved the Nationalist command in compromising situations. One such example involved the British ship *Cervantes*, an 1,810 ton vessel built in 1919 by H.& C. Grayson Ltd., in Garston (England), which belonged to Mac Andrews & Co. Ltd., London. This ship should not be confused with the Republican cruiser *Miguel de Cervantes*, 7,975 tons.

The British ship "Cervantes," which just managed to avoid a torpedo dropped by a Heinkel He 59.

The Republican cruiser "Miguel de Cervantes," which on occasion was confused with the British merchant vessel of the same name.

On the left is Admiral Bastarreche, who was Commandant General of Palma de Mallorca when the "Cervantes" incident occurred.

On 9 October the *Cervantes* was underway not far from Tarragona, steaming towards Valencia, when at 07:00 hours, some twelve miles from land, a Heinkel He 59 signalled the vessel by means of its searchlight that it should head for Palma de Mallorca. At first the ship followed the plane's instructions, but as the seaplane began to get further away it changed course and headed for Tarragona. The aircraft returned, this time dropping bombs that fell close to the ship, forcing it to set course again for Palma. Near mid-day, another Heinkel He 59 appeared and ordered the ship to head for Palma, a course that at this moment the vessel was already steering. Then the seaplane dropped an F 5 torpedo, which the captain of the merchant ship managed to skillfully avoid as it passed across his bow. Soon after this a Royal Navy destroyer, the HMS *Firedrake (H-79)*, appeared on the scene and escorted the merchant ship to safety in Valencia.

Following British protests, the then military commander of Palma de Mallorca, admiral Francisco Bastarreche, admitted "off the record" to the British consul in Palma, Mr. Hillgarth, that the seaplane pilot was German and that the aircraft had been carrying a torpedo. This admission was strictly against orders, and as a consequence admiral Bastarreche was arrested. Clearly, under no circumstances were the Nationalist commanders prepared to admit that their seaplanes were being flown by Germans and that, furthermore, these same crews were frequently contravening orders.

On 24 October, the French merchant vessel *Oued-Mellah* (ex *Cape St.Lucía*, ex *Junon*), 2,413 tons, built in 1918 by Jos. T. Eltringham & Co. Ltd., Willington Quay (England),

and belonging to the Compagnie de Navigation Pacquet, was attacked forty miles east of Barcelona by two Heinkel He 59s as it was en route from Casablanca to Port-Vendres, carrying a mixed cargo of cork, cereals, and minerals. The ship was hit by two bombs, one at the stern and another at the bow, without causing any casualties, and the ship sank that night. Two French warships, the *Milan* and *Le Mars,* came to the aid of the stricken ship and managed to save all the crew. The destroyer *Milan* was sent to Palma de Mallorca to protest the attack, but Admiral Moreno told the French representative that he had no knowledge of the attack and would carry out an investigation, and if necessary apply the pertinent sanctions.

The next day, the 73 ton French auxiliary vessel *Chasseur 91*, which belonged to Air France and was refuelling the seaplanes CAMS 53 and Lioré et Olivier LeO H. 242, operating the Marsailles-Algiers link, was sunk in the Republican port of Fornells (Menorca) by a Heinkel He 59, which machine-gunned and bombed the vessel. The boat was carrying ten thousand litres of fuel which caught fire, and the craft split in two and sank without casualties. The French destroyer *Le Mars* was sent to Mahon to investigate. Admiral Moreno informed the *Milan* that he would order the sinking of any ship anchored in that port.

The British merchant ship *Jean Weems* (ex *Lake Fluvanna*), of 2,349 tons, had been built in 1918 by the American shipyard S.B. Co of Cleveland, Ohio (United States), and was owned by the Thameside Ship Co London, which had recently acquired the vessel in New York and registered it in Gibraltar. The *Jean Weems* was sunk at 08:20 hours on 30 October, some fifteen miles from the coast, by a single Heinkel He 59 as it was steaming

An original framed photograph of a twin-engined Heinkel He 59 at Pollensa.

from Marsailles to Barcelona with a declared cargo of wheat, leather, and condensed milk. The ship had been chartered by the Republican government. The captain was British and the crew made up of various nationalties. On board were two observers from the Non-Intervention Committee (Gustav Obesom, of Swedish nationality, and Arnold Kilff, a Latvian). Before attacking the ship, the seaplane had made a pass overhead and identified eight trucks on its deck. The aircraft ordered the ship to halt and the crew to embark in the lifeboats. Then, the aircraft strafed the ship with its 20 mm cannon and dropped seventeen 50 kg bombs, of which four hit the target. The ship broke in two, and within ten minutes the stern section had disappeared beneath the waves. After five hours of rowing the twenty-six survivors reached Calella (Gerona), where they were attended to at one of the beach hotels.

The AS./88 operations report describes the attack as follows:

"At 0630 h, the 'Jean Weems' was spotted for the first time 15 miles east of cabo Bagur following a course of 240° at full steam ahead. The ship was carrying (what seemed to be cotton) 8 trucks painted grey green on one side, and flying the flag of Gibraltar.

Attack according to FT (radio) 2.5 cabo San Sebastián.

1) Repeated message: STOP, GO TO THE BOATS. Ship steering south.

2) Warning shots fired across the bow and order to halt repeated. The ship stopped and the crew took to the life boats.

3) Several strafing attacks made against the ship along the waterline and the cargo on the deck.

4) Bombs dropped on the stern with several hits scored. The ship sank after ten minutes. Crew in lifeboats, no other vessels sighted. Weather conditions: Bad visibility, clouds at 250 metres, Rain. In the rain the visibility down to less than one mile."

Close-up of a Rheinmetall Lb. 201 20 mm cannon with two twenty-round drum magazines, which was very effective against both ground and naval targets.

This action caused serious repercussions, both in the British press and Parliament. Angry protests were made to Burgos and in Palma de Mallorca, where the seaplane was based, although there was no mention that the plane had "spared" the crew. There was a heated exchange between vice admiral Andrew Cunningham and admiral Francisco Moreno. Finally, on 12 November, the Nationalist government admitted a mistake had been made, apologized for the sinking, and offered compensation. The British government was also given assurances that there would be no repetition of this type of attack against British merchant ships on the high seas.

At this time there were seven Heinkel He 59s at Pollensa numbered 522, 524, 525, 526, 528, 529, and 530, as well as a three-engined Ju 52/3m (527). All this would appear to indicate that the Heinkel He 59s numbered 521 and 523 were no longer operational. The Heinkel He 60s were still undergoing repairs.

November

The 643 ton French steamer *Le Corse* (ex *Fram*, ex *Monte Promina*), built in 1903 by W. Harkess & Son Ltd., Middlesbrough (England), and owned by Louis Carlini & Cie of Marsailles, had been on the list of vessels suspected of smuggling war materiel to the Republic since 1937. The ship had been chartered in Marsailles by the communist party to bring Yugoslavian volunteers for the International Brigades, but this plan fell through, and instead the ship was used to traffic arms to the Republic.

The French ship "Le Corse" was captured and renamed the "Castillo Jarandilla."

Two Heinkel He 59s over the Mediterranean coast.

According to the AS./88 operational report for 4 November, the vessel was spotted at 08:45 hours by two Heinkel He 59s carrying cargo some five miles northwest of the port of Barcelona. The seaplanes signalled the crew to abandon ship, which they did only after the aircraft had fired some warning shots and dropped a bomb ahead of the bow. The ship immediately shut down its engines and at the same time sounded its siren, as if calling for help from the nearby land. The Heinkel He 59s released several bombs that landed near the side of the ship, which appeared damaged and to be leaning slightly. During the bombing a Republican Polikarpov I-15 "Chato" fighter appeared on the scene and attacked the seaplanes; although it failed to down either of them, it did prevent the ship from being completely sunk. The French destroyers *Gerfaut* and *Vautour* arrived, which allowed the crew to reboard their vessel, and the destroyers escorted the *Le Corse* to Marsailles. A protest was sent to admiral Moreno, who replied that the ship was on the "black list" and that the attack had occurred within three miles from the coast.

The *Le Corse* was intercepted again some months later on 14 February 1939, together with the French yacht *Azelma*, and was forced into Barcelona port and seized before the French Navy could intervene on her behalf. In June 1940, the ship was handed over to the Shipping Office and renamed the *Castillo Jarandilla*. She was lost on 28 June 1943 when she caught fire in the port of Melilla.

On 26 November, a Heinkel He 59 arrived in Cadiz, via Melilla, without prior notice, causing the Balearic Air Regional Commander, Lieutenant Colonel Ramon Franco, to issue a complaint.

December

During this month, Republian fighter defenses began to appear with greater frequency around the targets; these aircraft consisted mainly of Russian Polikarpov I-15 “Chatos.”

According to Operations for AS./88 on 3 December, the previous day two Heinkel He 59s dropped ten 50 kg bombs on the rail line between Sagunto and Castellón. There was enemy anti-aircraft defense and they were attacked by three Republican Polikarpov I-15 “Chatos.”

That same day another two Heinkel He 59s were sent out on reconnaissance flights along the catalonian coast. The planes spotted a small vessel near Rosas but were attacked by three Polikarpov I-15 “Chatos,” although without consequences. They later spotted a British tanker leaving the port of Barcelona, where they were again intercepted by four Republican fighters defending the capital.

On the morning of 3 December, three Heinkel He 59s bombed the railway station and rail lines at Benicarlo, Oropesa, and Vinaroz. One of the Heinkel He 59s was attacked by two Polikarpov I-15 “Chatos,” causing serious damage to the Heinkel, but it was not shot down. However, the Republican government’s official war report of that day insists the Heinkel He 59 “*was shot down, fell into the sea and sank*.” This incident was a typical example of the manipulation of facts common to both sides in the conflict. This was particularly common when referring to enemy aircraft destroyed and one’s own losses. If all the claims made by both sides had been true, both would have been left without any aircraft by the middle of the conflict.

The Polikarpov I-15 “Chato” fighters of the Republican Air Force frequently intercepted the German seaplanes during their coastal incursions.

On 16 December, the Junkers Ju 52/3m (See) fitted with floats and numbered 527 took off for Melilla carrying the Nationalist poet Jose Maria Peman. At 16:30 hours the next day the plane returned to Pollensa.

A week later, on the 23rd, a Heinkel He 59 carried out a forced landing about a mile from the coast near Benicarlo due to damage sustained from Republican night-fighters. The crew were saved by the seaplane accompanying it. The damaged plane was then machine-gunned, set on fire, and sunk by the second seaplane according to the Germans, and by their own fighters according to the Republicans.

The AS./88 official report for the 24th states: "*Yesterday's operational report. At 06:15 hours two planes attacked the railway line and road between Oropesa and Benicarlo. One of the planes had to make an emergency landing two kilometres from the coast. The crew were picked up by the second plane. The plane in the water* (sic) *was set on fire and sunk. Three red fighters were present nearby but did not attack.*"

The official report by the Republican Ministry of Defense dated 23 December explains events as follows: "*A rebel seaplane shot down. At six fifteen, three seaplanes from Palma de Mallorca were flying near Peñíscola, where they dropped several bombs, as well as in Torre de Sal. Our fighters, which had run out of ammunition, returned to base and, once refuelled and rearmed, took off again and strafed the seaplane, which was still afloat, setting it on fire and destroying it.*"

During this period at the base at Pollensa there were a total of seven Heinkel He 59s (522, 524, 525, 526, 528, 529, and 530) operational, including the one recently arrived from Melilla, as well as the Junkers Ju 52/3m (W) fitted with floats (527). This last mentioned Heinkel He 59 was probably number 531.

A Heinkel He 59 suspended on a crane. The first emblems used by the Squadron can be seen at the front of the plane.

The "Ace of Spades" used by the Squadron from 1938 on.

6

The Blockade During the First Half of 1938. Main Air Operations and War Service of AS./88

January

In the middle of January, *Hauptmann* Hans Hefele returned to Germany and was relieved by *Hauptmann* Martin Harlinghausen, who became the fourth commander of AS./88 (January to December 1938), being promoted to *Major* in August of that year. In recognition of his outstanding service he was awarded the Spanish Military Medal Medalla Militar and the prestigious German *Deutsche Spanien-Kreuz in Gold mit Schwertern und Brillanten*.

Martin Harlinghausen was one of AS/88's most brilliant commanders.

A sequence of photographs showing a damaged Heinkel He 59 being recovered north of the base at Pollensa on 13 January 1938 following an accident in thick fog.

Another sequence showing the same damaged Heinkel He 59.

The first few days of January were marked by bad weather, which impeded operations.

On 13 January, a Heinkel He 59 crashed into the sea in the middle of heavy weather and thick fog north of Pollensa. *Unteroffizier/Flgz.-Mechaniker* Harald Kahl was drowned, and the rest of the crew were injured. The aircraft was lost. On the 15th, the coffin containing Kahl's remains was put aboard the three-engined Junkers Ju 52/3m (See) number 527 and taken to Cadiz, from where it was repatriated to Germany.

The AS./88 official report describes the incident as follows: "*AS/88. From 12 to 13.1, night sortie made by 5 He 59s against Port Bou. Note.- A He 59 of AS./88 was completely lost during landing* (sic) *caused by fog on the ground. The flight engineer was killed and the rest of the crew injured.*"

On the night 19 January, the Heinkel He 59 of *Hauptmann* Martin Harlinghausen, on one of its first missions, attacked the C.A.M.P.S.A. fuel tanks at the port of Valencia, causing a fierce fire. The crew were *Leutnant/Flugzeugführer* Volkmann Zenker, *Feldwebel* (radio) Josef Hinterberger, and *Leutnant* (flight engineer) Friedrich Schallmayer.

The AS./88 operational diary recorded the attack as follows: "*AS/88.*

One Heinkel He 59, on a sortie to CAMPSA in Valencia. Bombs successfully dropped on target. According to information received all of CAMPSA hit. Heavy destruction. Our reconnaissance aircraft observed thick smoke still over Valencia at 1200 hours. The bombing of Valencia has also been mentioned on radio Toulouse."

A CAMPSA fuel tanker hit during the bombing of the port of Valencia by Harlinghausen's He 59 on 19 January 1938.

The remains of a CAMPSA fuel tank in Valencia following an attack by AS./ 88.

The official War Diary of the Republican Ministry of Defense recorded the event, stating:

"*In the early hours of this morning Valencia was the target of two aerial bombardments. The first took place at 0149 hours and the second at 0517 hours. Considerable damage was caused in the city, however there were only a few casualties.*"Five days later, a note was attached to the AS./88 report stating the following: "*Sources indicate that the CAMPSA at Valencia was set on fire by an aircraft belonging to AS/88. No other aircraft were involved.*"

This dispelled some of the resentment felt by the German pilots that their successes were being attributed to aircraft from other formations, notably the Italian Legion's air component, which, as commented on by admiral Francisco Bastarreche, in his (Secret) report dated 02.10.37: "*When they are attributed with success it is necessary to put them in quarantine as their vanity and desire to negate and undervalue the performance of other units has led them to give false reports or claim the results of others as their own.*"

On the 28th, a Heinkel He 59 was forced to carry out a forced landing at sea north of Pollensa when it ran out of gasoline following a reconnaissance of the port of Mahon, on the Republican held island of Menorca. Due to the rough seas, the seaplane overturned and

Left, Admiral Francisco Bastarreche.

lost one of its floats. All members of the crew were rescued: one by a Nationalist Dornier *Wal* and others by the accompanying Heinkel He 59; and a fourth by the launch *Pollensa* belonging to AS./88, some two miles from Ciudadela. The aircraft was lost.

Above: Aerial view of the naval port of Mahon, on the Republican-held island of Menorca. Center and above: Photographs showing the state of a He 59 following a forced landing in rough seas near Ciudadela.

February

The 1,387 ton British ship *Alcira*, built in 1923 by L.Smit & Zoon, in Kinderdijk, Rotterdam (Holland), and belonging to J. Bruce & Co., registered in Glasgow, was sunk on 4 February by two Heinkel He 59s as it was steaming twenty miles from the coast, trying to enter the port of Barcelona. The ship had left Birmingham on 23 January with 1,800 tons of coal. On their first pass the seaplanes, flying at twenty-five metres, managed to hit the ship with three bombs, followed by another two on their next pass. Prior to attacking, the aircraft had signalled the crew to abandon ship and take to the lifeboats. The crew of twenty-five men, one of whom was injured, boarded a lifeboat, and were all rescued by the *Salvador*, a fishing boat out of Barcelona.

Alerted by their distress call, the commander of the Catalan anti-submarine defense flotilla immediately ordered the anti-submarine vessel *DAR I*, the *V-16 María* coastguard ship, and a Vickers *Vildebeest* seaplane to the area. When they arrived the *Alcira* had already been sunk, and the survivors were transferred aboard the *DAR 1,* which took them to Barcelona. Once there they were attended to at the base Flotilla and given food and clothing.

The Condor Legion report describes events as follows: "*This morning at 04:30 hours there was a reconnaissance patrol by two aircraft from San Sebastian to Barcelona. They attacked a ship attempting to enter the port of Barcelona some twenty miles from the coast, after ordering the crew to abandon ship. As the seaplanes approached the ship changed course and headed for the coast, proceeding to zig zag. The ship was sunk and the crew managed to escape in the lifeboats.*"

A Republican Vickers "Vildebeest" seaplane, like those of the coastal defense n° 71 Mixed Group.

Following protests from the British government, admiral Moreno claimed that the attack had taken place within three miles of the coast, but statements from the ship's captain, Mr. E.M. Osacker, the officer of the watch, David Hargnesa, and the control officer, Mr. Drysdale, clearly state that they were twenty miles from the coast. The incident gave rise to an exchange of diplomatic letters between the two countries, and the British Foreign Secretary, Anthony Eden, threatened reprisals without advanced warning if the incident was repeated, "*because his patience was not inexhaustable*."

The German pilot justified the attack by claiming he had mistaken the British ship for the Republican *Aldecoa*, which was reported to be on its way to Barcelona from Russia carrying war supplies. In the House of Commons, the British Prime Minister, Neville Chamberlain, stated that the Nationalist explaination was unsatisfactory, and that Her Majesty's government reserved the right to claim compensation.

Meanwhile, the 280 ton coastguard vessel *V-14 Rafael* (ex *Rafael Arcángel*, ex *Marie Richardson*), a fishing boat constructed in 1920 in Geestermande (Germany) that belonged to J. Botella and was flagged in Spain for Carranza in 1922 under the name *Rafael Arcangel*, was incorporated into the Catolonian anti-submarine flotilla when war broke out in July 1936. The vessel was armed with a Vickers 47/50 mm cannon at the bow and a Vickers 101.6/50 mm at the stern, as well as mounting a Vickers 7 mm anti-aircraft gun and carrying a number of depth charges.

It was getting late on 4 Februaary when the *V-14 Rafael* was patrolling the area near the entrance to the port of Barcelona, following the sinking that morning of the British merchant ship *Alcira*, which had been attacked by two Heinkel He 59s from AS./88. The

The crew of the "Alcira" were rescued and taken to Barcelona to the Coastal Defense Headquarters, where they were given food and clothing.

The 1,387 ton British ship "Alcira" was sunk two miles from the coast near the port of Barcelona.

commander of the patrolling vessel, who was to be wounded, identified the attacking seaplanes as friendly aircraft and did not open fire on them. At this time there were three Republican Vickers *Vildebeest* seaplanes moored at the wharf on the outer seawall at the port of Barcelona belonging to the Naval Air Service mixed nº 71 Group, cooperating with the anti-submarine flotilla. Perhaps this was the reason for the misidentification.

The 3,088 ton Republican Merchant ship "Aldecoa," which the German pilot of Heinkel He 59 had, it would seem, confused with the "Alcira."

Another view of a Republican Vickers "Vildebeest," this time painted with a camouflage scheme.

According to the operations report of AS./88 dated 5 February, events occurred as follows: "*A reconnaissance patrol was carried out at dusk last night along the Catalonian coast. Two thousand metres fom the entrance to the port of Barcelona, the guard ship 'Rafael' was attacked. There was anti-aircraft fire from the direction of Barcelona*."

The attack was confirmed by the Republican official war report of 4th February, which recorded that: "*Two seaplanes straffed the coastguard vessel "Rafael" near Prat without causing any casualties*."

On 11 February, a heavy storm with gusts of more than one hundred and twenty kilometres per hour swept the seaplane base at Pollensa for several hours. A Heinkel He 59 was seriously damaged, with both left-hand wings ripped out by the violence of the storm. It is possible that this un-numbered aircraft was written off as a result of the storm.

On 11 February 1938 the base at Pollensa was swept by a violent storm. The photograph shows one of the Heinkel He 59s that was seriously damaged with its left wings ripped off.

Another of the damaged seaplanes was this Cant Z-501 (62-4) of 2-G-62 Group, which fell off its carriage and suffered serious damage to its wings and hull.

Another Cant Z-501 (62-6) was found floating capsized. The reason the plane did not sink was because it did not have its engine fitted.

A Dewoitine D.371 monoplane of the Republican coastal defense fighter squadron nº 71 Group.

On 24 February, two Heinkel He 59s carried out a reconnaissance mission along the Catalan coast in search of the vessel *Río Segre*, which they were unable to find. About ten miles from San Sebastian the seaplanes were intercepted and attacked by three Republican Dewoitine D-371 fighters, although other sources claim they were Polikarpov I-15 "Chatos." One of the Heinkel He 59s received several hits. *Oberleutnant/Beobachter* Heinz Golcher was wounded by one of the rounds fired at the aircraft.

According to message nº 314, sent by Golcher at 10:45 hours on 26 February to the Nationalist Air Force Command, on the evening of 25 February the Heinkel He 59s, armed with four 250 kg bombs each, carried out an attack on two ships moored in the port of San Feliu de Guixols, sinking one un-named vessel of 250 tons. The AS./88 report detailed events further, stating: "*A fishing boat has been sunk*." This could have been the 60 ton *Castillo*, which was reported sunk at the end of the war.

The 2,265 ton Spanish cargo ship *Cabo Tres Forcas* was built in 1914 by Euskalduna de Construcción, of Bilbao; it was owned by Ybarra y Cía. of Seville, and in 1936 was one of the oldest and most prestigious ships in the Spanish merchant fleet. At the start of the war the ship was in the

Impacts from the machine gun of an enemy fighter in the wooden propeller of a Heinkel He 59.

Cantabrian Sea, but it also sailed the route to the Soviet ports in the Black Sea, transporting war materiel.

In the early hours of the morning of 26 February 1938, the *Cabo Tres Forcas* was moored in the port of San Feliú de Guixols. The vessel was hit by four of the eight 250 kg bombs dropped by two Heinkel He 59s of AS./88. The ship sank on its side. After the war, the *Cabo Tres Forcas* was refloated on 31 July 1941.

The operational diary of AS./88 for that day records the attack as follows: "*On 26.2. First sortie made by two He 59s against San Feliú. Two tons of bombs dropped. A ship hit with four bombs and sunk.*"

The Spanish freighter "Cabo Tres Forcas" was sunk at San Feliu de Guixols and refloated in July 1941.

Two SC 250 (250 kg) bombs. It was four of these that sank the "Cabo Tres Forcas."

March

Hauptmann Martin Harlinghausen sent message nº 331 at 14:46 hours on 5 March, asking the Nationalist Air Force Command for clarification as to whether the presence of a Royal Navy cruiser in the port of Barcelona at that time meant that it was prohibited to attack the port.

6 March 1938: The Nationalist cruiser Baleares sunk by the Republican fleet

That morning AS./88 sent several Heinkel He 59s on a reconnaissance mission over the exact area where the *Baleares* had been sunk, 65 miles from Cabo Palos on a course of 100º. Two Heinkel He 59s carried out a night sortie. Flying low, they attacked the Republican fleet anchored in the port of Cartagena with no result. The cruiser *Libertad* was moored on the La Curra jetty but was not hit.

The 1,003 ton Spanish mail ship *Isla de Menorca* (ex *Thesseus*) was built in 1883 by Forges & Chantiers of the Mediterranée, in La Seyne, Toulon (France), and was owned by the Valencian Trans-Mediterranean Company. The vessel participated in the evacuation of the Island of Ibiza by the Republicans in September 1936 and was in Tarragona at the end of that year being used as a prison ship. It was attacked on 14 March by two Heinkel He 59s near Cambrils while it was underway without cargo. The ship caught fire and headed towards the coast, where it ran aground at Mas de L´Arany and completely burned. It remained there until the end of the war, finally breaking up from the effects of the damage.

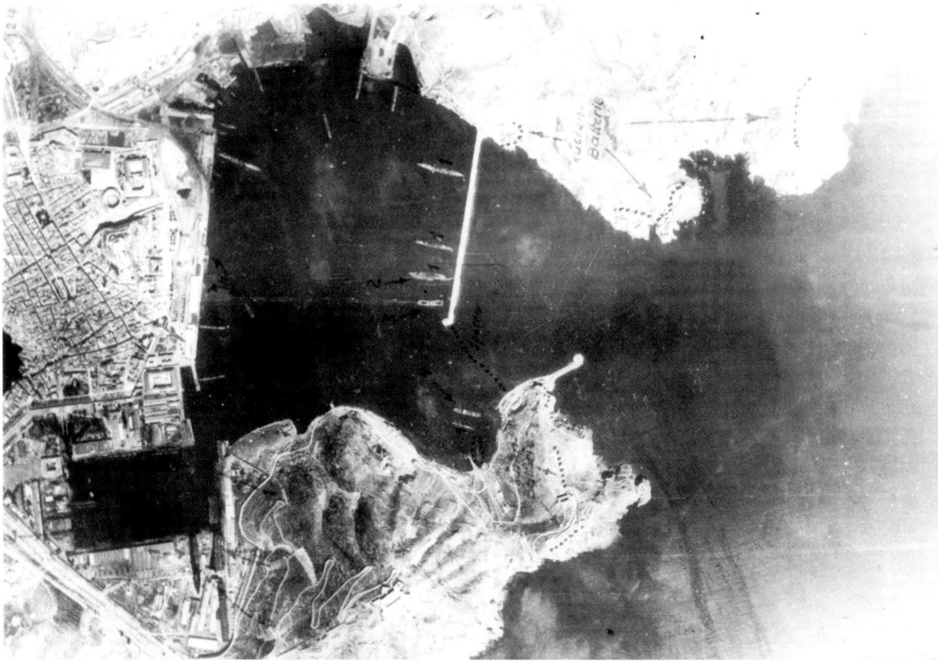

Aerial photograph of the port of Cartagena taken by a Condor Legion reconnaissance plane marking military targets.

The 757 ton British ship *Stanwel G.R.*, owned by Stanhope S.S. & Co. of London, was attacked at Tarragona at 04:30 hours on 15 March by a Heinkel He 59 that dropped two 250 kg bombs from low altitude, achieving a direct hit on the bridge and the engine room and causing a huge fire. Three men were killed, including the International Control officer, and another six were wounded. During the forty days the ship was in port undergoing repairs it was attacked by aircraft another fifteen times.

The AS./88 operations report for 14 to 15 March describes the event as follows: "*04:30 h. Two aircraft sent against railways and roads between Sagunto and Barcelona. The first aircraft dropped 2x250 kgs on a large ship (ignoring nationality and name) at Tarragona. Both bombs hit the ship causing explosions and fire. Destruction of vessel is assured.*"

The Note from the Republican Ministry of Defense confirmed the attack, saying: "*The ship which was set on fire yesterday in Tarragona by the rebel Air Force is the British Merchant ship 'Stanwel'. The fire started initially in both the bridge and the hold. The Tarragona fire brigade answered a call for help from the captain of the British vessel and were able to control the fire. Two dead and eight wounded. The dead and most of the wounded are of British nationality. Among the victims was the Danish officer representing the International Committee for non-intervention, who had stayed aboard the ship and has been seriously wounded.*" Two days later the sixty-two year old Danish officer, Masden, died from his wounds; he was a captain in the Danish merchant marine.

The damaged bridge of the British merchant ship "Stanwel" after being bombed by a Heinkel He 59 in the port of Tarragona.

Above: In the center of the photograph, wearing a white-crowned hat, is Captain Davis of the "Stanwel," surrounded by members of his crew. Below: Crew of the "Stanwel."

In the early hours of 15 March a Heinkel He 59 (529) of AS./88 received several hits from the 20 mm anti-aircraft gun mounted on a train near Vinaroz (Castellon), which forced the aircraft to make an emergency landing. The five crew members, who were uninjured, had time to set fire to the aircraft before they were taken prisoner and later exchanged.

Above: Sequence showing the remains of Heinkel He 59 number 529, which had to make a forced landing after being hit by fire from a Republican anti-aircraft train near Vinaroz. The first photograph shows the burned out wreckage of the seaplane. Below: The second picture shows the only part of the aircraft to survive the flames, the starboard float.

The crew was composed of *Oberfeldwebel* Rudolf Rücker, *Oberfeldwebel/Flugzeugführer* Alfred Tonollo, *Oberfeldwebel/Beobachter* Hermann Strohmaier, *Oberfeldwebel* Bruno Stötzer, and *Alferez Piloto* Jose Caetano Rocha Sepulveda Velloso, a Portuguese volunteer (member of Group 2 G-62) who was temporarily assigned to the German unit.

Above: The seaplane's crew, who were unhurt, were captured and later exchanged. Second from left is Tonollo; third, Strohmaier; and fourth, Stötzer. Below: Upper row, fourth from the left is Rücker. In the center of the bottom row is Sepúlveda Velloso, a Portuguese volunteer attached to AS./88.

The Note from the Republican Ministry of Defense described the shooting down of the seaplane as follows: "*In the early hours of this morning at four thirty, a seaplane coming form Palma de Mallorca descended on Vinaroz, first strafing the road between that town and Benicarlo. Having discovered a train moving between Vinaroz and Ulldecona, the seaplane began an attacking run, but the train's anti-aircraft defenses succeeded in hitting the aircraft and brought it down. The rebel plane, which was crewed by three Germans* (sic), *fell in flames some three kilometres from Vinaroz, near the San Carlos de La Rapita road.*"

The AS./88 operational report for 17 to 18 March records that: "*At 00:15 h. Ship of approx 1,000 tons attacked 1 km north of the port of La Selva, with 5x50 kgs. All bombs on target. Ship set on fire and run aground.*"

A Heinkel He 59 of AS./ 88 dropping five 50 kg bombs on the port of La Selva.

The attack was confirmed by the Republican Maritime Mobile Defense, which stated that during that day the Republican coastguard ships *V-10 Ana* and *V-16 Maria* were trying to refloat a Greek ship, hoping to get her off the rocks and beach her near the port of La Selva. The vessel in question was the Greek *Navarion*, which was carrying war materiel from La Nouvelle to Barcelona.

At 01:20 hours that same day, the Spanish sailing ship *San Silverio*, of 60 tons, was sunk at the port of San Felíu de Guixols, after being hit by one of ten 50 kg bombs dropped by a Heinkel He 59 of AS./88. The AS./88 operational report commented: "*At 01:20 h. 10x50 kg bombs dropped on sailing ship at San Feliu. One bomb on target.*"

In the early hours of 21 March, three Heinkel He 59s made a night sortie and dropped three tons of bombs from 2,800 metres on the railway bridge and station at Tortosa. The bombs hit their targets and the planes then flew off at low altitude. One of the aircraft did not return to its base at Pollensa. At 05:00 hours, according to Radio Barcelona,

German SC 50 (50 kg) bomb.

the missing seaplane had been shot down by a Republican night-fighter near Cambrils. The crew was composed of *Oberleutnant/Beobachter* Hayo Jürgens, *Leutnant/Flugzeugführer* Karl Zunker, and *Unteroffiziers* Kurt Keitzel and Kurt Werner. Three burned to death in the plane and the other died from his wounds soon after. The Republicans credited pilot Jose Sarrio Calatayud of nº 71 mixed Group, flying a Dewoitine D. 510 TH, with the victory, and the Ministry of Defense promoted him to Lieutenant. Other sources attribute the destruction of the seaplane to an exploding ammunition truck it had just attacked, but the fact is it was

Remains of a Heinkel He 59 of AS./88 shot down by a Republican Dewoitine D-510 at Cambrils in which all the crew burned to death.

One of the two Republican Dewoitine D-510 monoplane fighters in nº 71 Mixed Group. One of them shot down a Heinkel He 59 on the night of 21 March 1938.

brought down by a Republican fighter. The information bulletin of the commander of the 4th Sector of the 3rd Air Region (Barcelona) describes the event as follows:

"*At 04:25 h, with enemy aircraft known to be in the vicinity of Reus, a Dewoitine took off from this aerodrome and engaged two enemy seaplanes at Cambrils, shooting down one of them which fell on the Cambrils to Hospitalet road, killing three of its four crew, the remaining airmen was taken to Hospital in Cambrils, where he died 40 minutes later. It would appear he was of German nationality. It seems the aircraft is the same as the one which was brought down at Vinaroz (a twin-engined Heinkel seaplane). The aircraft was completely destroyed.*

The other seaplane was forced to drop its bombs at sea, and then disappeared in the direction of Palma; our fighter could not follow as it had run out of ammunition. The Dewoitine D-510 TH, number CW-001, piloted by Sargeant Sarrio, returned at 04:55 h, landing at Reus with no further incident."

Also on the 21st, the AS./88 Junkers Ju 52/3m (See) with floats fitted was attacked as it returned from Cadiz to Pollensa, near Cartagena, by two Fiat CR. 32 "Chirri" fighters that had been captured by the Republicans and flown from their base at Los Alcazares (Murcia). The Junkers Ju 52 was hit in its fuel tank and one of the crew was slightly wounded, which caused it to make a stop at Formentera; following repairs it continued on to Pollensa. The AS./88 report does not mention it, but the machine guns mounted in the three-engined Junkers Ju 52/3m (W) managed to shoot down one of the attacking aircraft. However, the operational report of the Republican Coastal Defense records the incident as follows:

"At 15:10 h, two fighters took off to intercept an enemy seaplane spotted eight miles from the coast, north-east of Cabo Palos. The fighters engaged the enemy aircraft but the rebel managed to shoot down one of our planes, which landed in the sea thirty-five kilometres from the coast west of Cabo Palos. The plane exploded on impact and disappeared under the waves along with its pilot.

The enemy plane, a single-engined (sic) *monoplane with floats, disappeared from view, but seemed to have been hit, according to the report of the remaining fighter pilot.*"

The Republican Air Force Staff bulletin records the moment in which Air Force Commander Hidalgo de Cisneros congratulates Sargeant José Sarrió Calatayud for shooting down the He 59.

Fuerzas Aéreas
ESTADO MAYOR
2ª SECCION

30 MARZO 1938 BOLETIN DE INFORMACION N.º 3

HÉROES DE LA "GLORIOSA"

EL JEFE DE LAS FUERZAS AÉREAS FELICITA AL NUEVO TENIENTE SARRIÓ CALATAYUD

EL HEINKEL 59 DERRIBADO EN VUELO NOCTURNO POR EL SARGENTO SARRIO CALATAYUD

Rare photograph of the only Junkers Ju 52/3m W in AS/88, fitted with floats and numbered 527. The aircraft's gunner managed to shoot down a Fiat CR.32 off the coast of Cartagena.

The pilot of the downed Republican Fiat CR. 32 was Sargeant Vicente Gay Gomez, who was killed.

Curiously, the AS./88 operational report for the 23rd confirmed the attack but not that the aircraft had been shot down, stating: "*AS/88. 21.3, during the transfer flight of a Ju 52 of AS/88 from Cadiz to Pollensa, the aircraft was attacked by two enemy fighters. A soldier was slightly wounded.*"

This same day saw a Heinkel He 59 from Cadiz made operational at Pollensa to replace the plane shot down; the next day a Heinkel He 60 was put into service at the base.

The Republican Air Force used captured Fiat CR.32s in coastal defense and at the fighter school.

April

The Spanish tug *Río Urumea*, 276 tons, had been built in 1929 by N.V. Schpsw (Holland) and belonged to Puertos y Pantanos de Barcelona SA. This vessel had been assigned to coastguard duty and given the number *V-13* in the Catalan Anti-submarine Flotilla. The tug was armed with a Vickers 76.2 mm at the bow and another 47 mm gun at the stern, as well as a Vickers 7 mm anti-aircraft machine gun and a number of depth charges. At 20:45 hours on 7 April, the tug was attacked while she was returning from escorting the *S.A.C.-7* from Barcelona to the French frontier by a Heinkel He 59 that dropped twenty 50 kg bombs from 800 metres. She had moored in the port of Rosas, next to the *V-16 María*. Four men aboard the *V-16* were killed, the pier was badly damaged, and the *V-13 Rio Urumea* sunk. The tug was refloated on 9 April 1940 and used as a cargo transporter.

The report of the Balearic Islands Regional Air Force Command (Section 2 Information) describes the attack: "*Operations 7-4-38: 20:45 h. One aircraft dropped 20x50 kg bombs from 800 m on a ship moored in the port of Rosas, hitting both the dock and the ship. Three searchlights and anti-aircraft fire*."

15 April 1938: Nationalist troops reach the Mediterranean

At 20:25 hours on 22 April, a Heinkel He 59 dropped a 500 kg bomb from 150 metres on a ship near the port of Sagunto, achieving a direct hit. The other 500kg bomb landed near the side of the vessel. There was a heavy defensive response, including anti-aircraft fire and searchlights.

The Spanish tug "Río Urumea" sunk by AS./ 88 in the port of Rosas.

Group of German SC 50 bombs.

The AS./88 official report for the 23rd had the following entry added: "*The Palma Naval Section informs that the destroyer hit yesterday by AS/88 in Sagunto was the seaplane carrier 'Dedaldo'* (sic)."

Obviously the report is referring to the seaplane carrier *Dedalo* (ex *Neuenfels*), constructed in 1901 by Swan Hunter & Wigham Richardson & Co. Ltd. at their shipyard in Newcastle (England). Interned in Vigo in 1914, it was transferred to the Spanish government as the *España Nº 6* as compensation for losses incurred by U-Boat action during the First World War. Following its conversion it was renamed the *Dedalo* and entered service with the Spanish navy in 1922 as a seaplane carrier for the naval air service. The ship had a displacement of 5,650 tons. The vessel saw service in the first campaign of the Moroccan war and the landing at Alhucemas. It had been left anchored near the port of Sagunto, waiting to be scrapped. The aviation historian Luis Ignacio Azaola showed some time ago that the sinking was mentioned in the notebooks of *Leutnant* Franz Brey.

The Spanish seaplane carrier "Dédalo" was sunk by AS./ 88 in Sagunto.

Two German SC 500 bombs on PVC 505 external carriers.

A Heinkel He 60 of AS./ 88 forced down near Vinaroz (Castellon).

On the morning of 26 April, the only Heinkel He 60 belonging to AS./88 had been obliged to moor near Vinaroz, returning to its base in Pollensa the following day.

AS./88 bombed traffic and communications in the vicinity of Vendrell and Benicassim in the early hours of 30 April. Due to the low altitude of the attacking aircraft, a 250 kg bomb caused damage to one of the Heinkel He 59s as it exploded. This incident is noted in the AS./88 operations report for 2 May: "*On 30th April serious damage to Heinkel He 59 AS/88 caused by premature detonation of 250 kg bomb. No losses incurred.*" Losses obviously referred to human life, but the aircraft itself was so seriously damaged that it was probably written off.

May

According to the Condor Legion's official dispatch, in the early hours of 17/18 April four He 59s bombed the port of Castellon two times at low altitude, dropping four 250 kg bombs. The bombs sank a sailing boat and damaged the tugs *D-130* and *D-131*, and caused damage to sheds on the wharf. On this date the chief of the Condor Legion stayed overnight in the Balearic Region.

At 03:00 hours on 22 May, a solitary Heinkel He 59 dropped four 250 kg bombs fom a height of eighty metres on the port of Torrevieja, with one bomb hitting its target. This was the motor-sailing vessel *Adela Villanueva* of 300 tons, carrying a cargo of wheat in its hold.

A Heinkel He 59 carrying four 250 kg SC 250 bombs. It was one of these bombs that exploded prematurely while a Heinkel He 59 was making a low level attack.

However, the ship was not completely sunk thanks to the rapid and heroic action of her engineer, who had been sleeping aboard the vessel, who started her engines and beached her in order to save her.

Also, at 03:50 hours on 22 May a Heinkel He 59 dropped two 500kg bombs from eighty metres on a merchant ship in the port of Alicante, hitting the target. There was a large explosion and the unknown ship sank.

The British merchant ship *Thorpehall* (ex *Bazan*, ex *Oakmere*) of 1,251 tons, built in 1910 by Sunderland Ship Building Co. Ltd., Sunderland (England), and belonging to Westcliff Shipping Co. Ltd. of London, who was determined to take advantage of the opportunities for trafficking arms. The ship was built in 1936 with 1,000 pounds sterling of capital by the Greeks Pandelis and Katepodis and Gordon Till (who contributed two pounds), the main instigator of this and other similar enterprises. His fleet consisted of four ships: *Thorpebay*, *Thorpehall*, *Thorpeness*, and *Thorpehaven*, the last three all sunk by Heinkel He 59s of AS./88.

The known contraband vessel *Thorpehall*, protagonist in some well known incidents in the northern campaign, multiplied its voyages to the east coast of Spain. At 03:50 on 25 May the ship was sunk by a solitary Heinkel He 59, which dropped two 500 kg bombs from an altitude of fifty metres when the ship had anchored, with her lights out, in the Gulf of Valencia, a mile from the port. The ship had arrived from Marsailles carrying wheat and war materiel. As it began its attack the seaplane was engaged by searchlights and anti-aircraft fire.

Patrol of three Heinkel He 59s on a reconnaissance and bombing mission.

The Greek tanker "Nausicaa" was bombed and sunk in Menorcan waters.

The AS./88 report for the day ends with the phrase "see note overleaf," which read: "*Two 500 kg bombs fell near the stern of the ship. According to German press reports the ship is the British 'Thorpehall,' which sank.*"

This information was confirmed by the Republican Ministry of Defense on 26 May: "*The port of Valencia was also attacked yesterday with five bombs hitting and sinking the British ship 'Thorpehall'. The ship's first officer was badly wounded as well as the International Control officer, an Irish citizen.*"

According to AS./88, on 27 May a 1,500 ton vessel was sunk at Grao de Castellon.

The Greek tanker *Nausicaa* (5,005 tons) was built in 1922 by N of Ireland S.B. Co. Ltd. of Londonderry (Northern Ireland). The ship belonged to K.E. Veniselos of Pireo, later transferring ownership to Burlington S.S. Co. of London, where it was renamed *Burlington*. The ship made several voyages to Russia under both names in order to transport petroleum to Republican ports. It was siezed by the Italian cruiser *Barletta* in 1937 and taken to Palma as it was on its way from the Black Sea with 7,000 litres of petroleum, which was confiscated. The ship was released following British protests.

Nevertheless, nine months later the vessel's luck was to change. On 27 May 1938 the ship was spotted twenty miles south of Menorca, off the port of Mahon. Immediately, the Heinkel He 59 commanded by *Leutnant* Franz Brey took off with another four Heinkel He 59s and attacked the *Nausicaa*, dropping twenty 250 kg bombs from 50-100 m altitude. The ship received eleven hits, the explosions setting the vessel completely on fire. The tanker sank the next day, the crew being rescued by the Italian merchant ship *Securitas*, which was heading for Genova.

Brey was the only officer of AS./88 awarded one of the highest Spanish decorations, the Individual Military Medal, which he received from General Franco in person on 12 May 1939 at Barajas airport (Madrid).

Two days later, according to the operations report of the German Naval Mission in Palma dated 29/30 May, at 21:45 hours on 29 May a Heinkel He 59 dropped two 500 kg bombs fitted with delayed fuses from fifty metres on a ship moored at the north pier at the port of Valencia. The bombs fell two to five metres from the side of the ship, having an effect like a mine and setting the ship on fire. The vessel was towed out of the port and the crew were rescued. The ship was the 2,575 ton French cargo ship *El Djem* (ex *Draa*, ex *Phu-Yen*), built in 1902 by Craig, Taylor & Co. in Stockton (England) and owned by Soc. Maritime Nationale of Paris and later chartered by France-Navigation, The vessel had arrived in Valencia from La Nouvelle carrying fuel. The French government did not protest because the ship was outside the established "security zone," and its stay in the port was entirely at its own risk.

The 1,988 ton British merchant ship *Penthames* (ex *Comtesse de Flandre*, ex *Neva*) was built in 1909 by Clyde S.B. & E. Co. Ltd. in Port Glasgow (United Kingdom), and was owned by Pentirinion S.S. Co. Ltd. (D.P. Barnett) of London. The vessel was bombed and sunk during the early hours of 30/31 May by two Heinkel He 59s while it was anchored a mile off Valencia. As the ship had been sunk outside the port the German pilot was suspended for disobeying orders and returned to Germany in the face of British protests.

The official AS./88 report describes the event as follows: "*AS/88. 30th/31st, four He 59s, night sortie against port of Valencia. Four tons. 50 to 1,800 metres. Ship and breakwater hit. Fire observed.*"

The sinking was confirmed by the Republican official report for 1 June, which stated: "*In one of the agressions perpetrated against the port of Valencia two nights ago, one of the rebel planes managed to fly over the port installations and drop its bombs, which resulted in the sinking of the British merchant ship 'Penthanes'* (sic)-*London.*"

The British merchant ship "Penthames" was sunk in the port ofValencia.

Above: A BMW VI U aero-engine with propeller differential, like those fitted to the Heinkel He 59 seaplanes. Below: Another BMW VI U, this time without the propeller differential. These engines were also fitted to the He 59s.

A German SC 250 kg bomb now exhibited in the Cuatro Vientos Air Museum (Madrid).

A group of German SC 50 kg bombs photographed in the same museum

A Babcock & Wilcox crane, made in Bilbao under licence and used as a hoist for the seaplanes of AS./88 in Pollensa (Mallorca).

An unexploded SC 250 kg bomb recovered from the port of Valencia.

Memorial at the seaplane base in Pollensa, erected in memory of those German airmen of AS./88 killed in action during the Spanish Civil War. The names of those killed in the accident of 1.1.1939 are missing.

Obverse and reverse of the ensign used by the Condor Legion in Spain.

Memento signed by several of the commanders and officers of AS./88 in Pollensa.

Heinkel He 60 number 512, known as "La Fiera del Mar" (the Sea Beast). (Ilustration; UriARTE)

Heinkel He 60 number 515. Both seaplanes bore the skull and crossbones emblem of the German seaplane unit. (Ilustration: UriARTE)

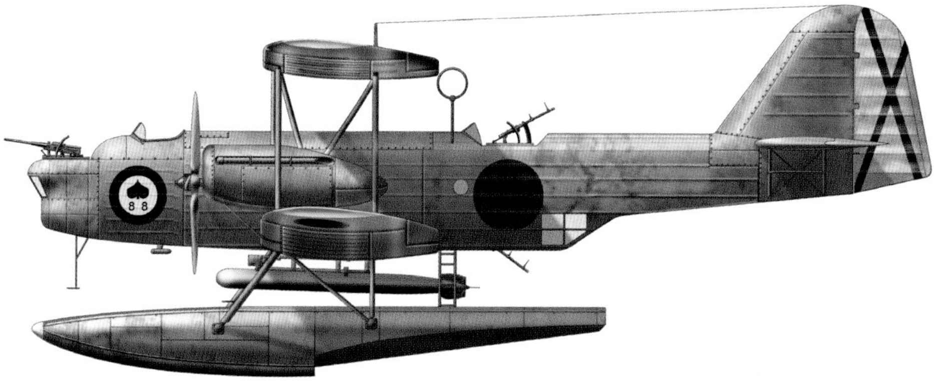

A Heinkel He 59 bearing an unusual version of the ace of spades emblem on its nose. (Illustration: UriARTE)

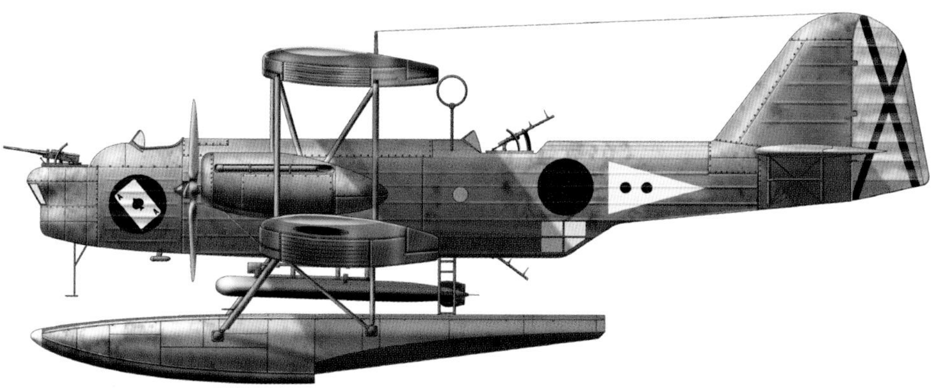

A Heinkel He 59, this time with the definitive version of the AS./88 squadron emblem, the ace of spades, as well as the Non- Intervention pennant on the fuselage. Both planes are armed with Horten torpedos. (Illustration: UriARTE)

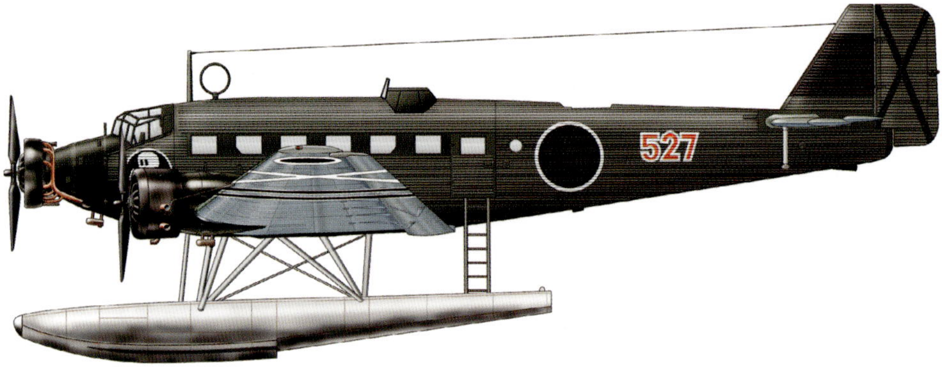

Junkers Ju 52 3m (W) number 527. This aircraft was used by AS./88 for liaison and transport missions. (Ilustration: UriARTFI)

Heinkel He 115. This was the most advanced type of seaplane in service with AS./88 in the closing stages of the Spanish Civil War. (Ilustration: Julio L. Caeiro)

June

The dispatch sent by the Condor Legion to the Balearic Regional Air Command regarding the operations carried out by AS./88 on the night of 3/4 June mentions that at 22:40 hours on the 3rd, a solitary Heinkel He 59 dropped four 250 kg bombs and fourteen incendiaries from an altitude of one hundred metres on a ship in the port of Alicante, with three bombs hitting the ship and one the pier. The bombs caused a large fire. The aircraft encountered anti-aircraft fire and searchlights.

At 00:35 hours on 4 June the now burning vessel was attacked again by another Heinkel He 59. Again four bombs were dropped, but this time from one thousand metres, resulting in one bomb hitting the ship and another striking the pier. There was anti-aircraft fire as before. The ship that had been attacked was the British tanker *Maryad*, and four men aboard the vessel were killed.

This attack was confirmed on the one hand by the Republican official report for the 4th as follows: "*In the early hours of today a rebel plane launched an attack on Alicante, but was repulsed by our anti-aircraft batteries. The aircraft dropped its bombs on the British ship 'Maryat,' setting it on fire and killing four of its crew.*"; and on the other in the report issued by the German Naval Mission in Palma, which said: "*The ship bombed in Alicante on 3rd of this month at 22:40 was the British tanker 'Marryat.' The vessel has been left burning in the port.*"

German 10kg B 1 incendiary, like the fourteen dropped on the British tanker "Maryad" as she lay moored in the port of Alicante.

The small Spanish freighter *Frutero* (ex *Normand*, ex *Bell Rock*), 340 tons, was built in 1893 by R. Willi & Son of Workington (England), and was owned by Jose Llovet-Ball y Hermanos of Valencia. According to the AS./88 report for 7/8 June, on that night it was attacked three times in succession by three of the Squadron's Heinkel He 59s. The first attack occurred at 21:45 hours on 7 June and was made by a Heinkel He 59 that dropped four 250 kg bombs from a height of fifty metres, just off the coast from Benicasim. None

The Spanish freighter "Frutero" was bombed several times by Heinkel He 59s of AS./ 88 and forced to run aground by 20mm cannon fire near Benicasim.

of the bombs hit the target. The plane used its Rheinmetall L.b. 201 20 mm cannon to force the ship to run aground. The ship's crew returned fire with light machine guns and rifles, hitting the seaplane several times. Two hours later another He 59 arrived and dropped twenty 50 kg bombs from 300 metres. Two of the bombs hit the ship, which was also strafed. Finally, at 03:15 on the 8th a third He 59 dropped another four 250 kgs bombs from eighty metres, with three hitting the vessel, seriously damaging it. The freighter was recovered after the war.

The 3,688 ton British merchant vessel *Thorpehaven* (ex *Essex Jugde*, ex *Bainsizza*, ex *Alberto Fassio*, ex *Antium*, ex *Daghestan*) was built in 1912 by Short Bros Ltd., of Sunderland (England). The ship belonged to Westcliff Ship Co. of London, which was taking advantage of the war to do business, as has already been mentioned. At 22:20 hours on 7 June the vessel was sunk by a Heinkel He 59, which dropped two 500 kg delayed fuse bombs on its deck from a height of fifty metres when it was anchored near the port of Alicante, after having arrived from Marsailles with three thousand tons of wheat. One of the two bombs hit the ship and the other struck the pier. The seaplane also dropped a further five 50 kg bombs on a second ship, which hit its side. There was heavy anti-aircraft fire and searchlights, and the plane returned to base having received several impacts.

The Republican official war report for 8 June described events as follows: "*In the early hours of yesterday morning two enemy aircraft flew in from Mallorca and dropped several bombs on the port of Alicante, hitting the British vessels 'Thorpehaven' and 'English Tanker'.../...*"

A Heinkel He 59 preparing to land after carrying out a mission over the Mediterranean.

At the end of the war the *Thorpehaven* was found aground on a beach near the port of Alicante. The ship had an enormous six by seven-metre hole on its starboard side, astern of the engine room, affecting the door to the same and hold number three. The hole was covered with a single panel and the engine room and holds were pumped out. The ship had been loaded with three thousand tons of wheat, which obstructed the bombs and made the task of pumping difficult. The wheat was used for fertiliser, animal food, and making starch.

The ship was refloated on 27 September 1939 by the Commision for Salvaging Ships, and was taken to Bilbao to be rebuilt. In November 1941 the vessel was incorporated into the Administration and renamed *Castillo Guadalest* and given over to the Aznar shipping company of Bilbao. In 1943 the vessel was acquired by the Elcano National Company. On 15 September 1951 the ship began taking on water and sank some 600 miles northwest of Bermuda, on a voyage from Bilbao to Boston. The crew were rescued by a Honduran merchant ship.

The British *English Tanker* (ex *Oilfield*), of 6,170 tons displacement plus 2,000 ton carrying capacity, was built in 1923 by the Tyne Ship Building Co. Ltd., Newcastle (England). She was the property of the Compañía Arrendataria del Monopolio de Petróleos Sociedad Anónima (C.A.M.P.S.A.) de Madrid, which in 1936 had a magnificent modern fleet of tankers, all of which had been built in Spanish shipyards. During the war the company acquired three more ships from abroad, flying flags of conveniance in order to assure their provisioning. Among these vessels was the *English Tanker*, acquired from the Mid-Atlantic Shipping Co.

The British merchant ship "Thorpehaven" was sunk in the port of Alicante.

The attacks made by Heinkel He 59s on Republican ports led to several "notorious" successes.

At 23:20 hours on 7 June, the *English Tanker* was attacked by a Heinkel He 59 that dropped four 250 kg bombs and several incendiaries on the ship as it lay at anchor in the port of Alicante. The four bombs hit the tanker, causing extensive damage and fire. The seaplane was met with searchlight-directed anti-aircraft fire. The vessel was refloated on 26 April 1939, and the fuel still contained in her tanks was extracted. In August 1940 she was passed on to the Merchant Shipping Administration and renamed the *Castillo Almenara*, towed to Valencia, and repaired at the Union Naval de Levante shipyard. She returned to service in June 1942. On 22 March 1945, then renamed *Camposines*, she was returned to CAMPSA. The vessel was scrapped in 1967.

The British "English Tanker" was sunk in the port of Alicante.

The British dredger "Gandía" was sunk by Heinkel He 59s of AS. /88 in the port of the same name.

Also on the night of 7 June, AS./88 made two attacks on the port of Gandia. The first, at 22:00 hours, was by a single He 59 that dropped seven 50 kg bombs from an altitude of 250 metres on the sheds and warehouses on the docks, which caused four large explosions and damaged the motor-sailing ship *Cala Fornells* (93 tons), the property of Naviera Mallorquina S.A. of Palma de Mallorca, which was soon repaired. Five minutes later another He 59, perhaps the same one, dropped thirteen more 50 kg bombs on another ship, four of which found their target, setting the vessel on fire. This was the 316 ton dredger *Gandia*, built in 1891 in Glasgow (Scotland) and property of the British "Alcoy-Gandia Railway and Harbour Co. Ltd.," which was found sunk next to the coal jetty at the end of the war. Refloated on 13 June 1940, she was sold for scrap.

Frontal view of the robust Heinkel He 59.

The French freighter *Brisbane* (4,004 tons) was built in 1909 and was owned by André Puech of Paris, who in 1938 decided to run the risk of participating in the traffic of merchant shipping in the Mediterrnean. The ship transported a cargo of fertiliser and amonia sulphate from Algeria to Denia, where she was attacked four times by AS./88 as she lay at anchor in the aforementioned port.

According to the AS./88 operations report, the first attack took place at 22:30 hours 8 June, when a Heinkel He 59 dropped four 250 kg bombs from an altitude of eighty metres, with only one hitting the target. Another He 59 returned an hour later, strafing and dropping another four 250 kg bombs and several incendiaries and managing to hit the target with one of them and starting a fire in the stern, killing five of the crew and wounding another thirteen, among them the captain of the ship. The ship was seriously damaged, with its deck riddled with bullet holes and taking in water, resulting in it having to be run aground. The following day two French destroyers, one of which was the *Frondeur*, arrived in Denia and, after attending the burial of the victims, transported the surviving members of the crew to Algeria.

The Republican official war report for 9 June confirmed the attack: "*At 22:42 hours yesterday (8th), a rebel seaplane flew over the port of Denia at seven hundred metres dropping five bombs on the French merchant ship 'Brisbane', setting it on fire at the stern. The ship was also strafed. Five men were killed, four of the crew and the international observer and thirteen were wounded, including the ship's captain.*" The local Alicante newspaper, "Nuestra Bandera," dated 10 June, published a list of the dead: Edward Jones, observer for International Non-intervention Committee, British; William Bullock, purser, British; Henri Glaufer, second pilot, French; Yia Ben Hamon, oarsman, French; and Yan Vechini, stoker, French.

The French freighter "Brisbane," seen here in the foreground, was sunk by AS./ 88 in the port of Denia.

A Heinkel He 59 landing at its base after returning from a mission.

The third and fourth attacks occurred on the night of 13 June. According to the AS./88 operations diary, three Heinkel He 59s made a low level attack on the *Brisbane* in two waves, one at 22:40 and another an hour later. The aircraft dropped fifteen 50 kg bombs, four 250 kg, and two 500 kg bombs (*m.V., mit Verspätung*, or with delayed fuses). 70% hit the target, exploding and setting the vessel on fire. The port defenses responded with anti-aircraft machine-gun fire and all three aircraft received impacts. Curiously, it appears possible that one of the 500kg bombs that missed the *Brisbane* was found on 27 January 2008 by members of a Denia diving club.

The Republican government's official war record for 14 January describes the action as follows: "*At 23:30 a rebel seaplane flew over Denia and attacked the French merchant ship 'Brisbane', hitting her with two bombs and setting her on fire.*"

The 1,324 ton British ship *Isadora* (ex *SNA 2*, ex *Espelette*) was built in 1915 by G. Brown & Co., Greenock (Scotland), for John Kelly Ltd. The vessel was later sold to Rolfe & Stone Ltd., based in the port of Lavelly (Northern Ireland). This shipping company had a fleet of ten coasters, of which at least three shipped arms in the Cantabrian and Mediterranean seas.

According to the AS./88 operations diary, the *Isadora* was attacked on two consecutive days as she was moored in the port of Castellon unloading wheat brought from Marsailles. The first attack occurred at 21:45 hours on 8 June, and was carried out by a Heinkel He 59 that dropped four 250 kg bombs from an altitude of one hundred metres, two of which hit their target. During the same attack the seaplane strafed and sank a sailing vessel. This was the 169 ton *Pascual Flores*, built in 1918 and owned by E. Formiga Clapes, of Alicante. It was refloated and recovered after the war.

Above is a photograph of the British ship "Isadora" and in the lower is the wooden packet "Pascual Flores," both sunk in the same action by Heinkel He 59s of AS./ 88 in the port of Castellón.

A Heinkel He 59 begins its take off run from the base at Pollensa.

The second attack came at 22:45 on 9 June when another Heinkel He 59 dropped a further three 250 kg bombs on the already badly damaged *Isadora* from one hundred metres, as well as several incendiaries, two of them hitting the ship, which sank. The Republican official war report for 10 June confirmed the sinking: "*At 23:16 yesterday, a 'Saboya'* (sic) *seaplane attacked the British merchant ship 'Isadora', bombing and sinking her.*" (Note to reader: as can be seen, the times recorded in the Nationalist reports are different from those of the Republicans. Generally speaking the Nationalist entries are an hour behind.)

The ship was refloated in 1940, and handed over to the Administration in May 1941 under the name *Castillo Frías*. In July 1943 she was transferred to the Elcano National Company. In February 1959 she was bought by Ason of Santander and renamed *Deimos*. After fifty-three years of sea service she was scrapped in Gijon in 1968.

Meanwhile, at 21:45 on 9 June, a Heinkel He 59 dropped five 50 kg bombs and several incendiaries on sheds at the port of Gandia, causing a large fire. The seaplane also dropped two 500 kg bombs on two vessels moored in the port, sinking a sailing ship. This was the *Cala Portals* (ex *Capitan Angelats*, ex *Pi C.1*) of 130 tons, built in 1918 in Palma de Mallorca and the property of Naviera Mallorquina S.A. The ship was immediately taken out of the water, repaired, and returned to service.

A beached Heinkel He 59.

The AS./88 operations diary for 12 June reveals that the Heinkel He 59s began daytime flights at this time, adding to the risk to both crews and aircraft.

The 4,798 ton British *Thorpeness*, built in 1914 and belonging to Westcliff Ship & Co of London, established in 1936 with a view to trafficking armament, was attacked at 21:50 hours on 21 June by Heinkel He 59 number 530, using a F 5 torpedo as it made its way from Marsailles. The ship had anchored in the Gulf of Valencia with its lights out, with a cargo of wheat and other material aboard.

The Spanish sailing ship "Cala Portals" sunk in Gandía.

The British vessel "Thorpeness" torpedoed by a Heinkel He 59 piloted by Harlinghausen in the Gulf of Valencia.

The F 5 torpedo was successfully employed in the Spanish Civil War on two occasions: against the Danish merchant ship "Edith" and the British "Thorpeness."

What follows is the detailed entry describing this mission included in the AS./88 weekly (secret) report for 20 to 26 June 1938, which was sent to *Hauptmann* Harlinghausen at Sonderstab "W" in Berlin:

"*21.06.38 Flying order: 1 Torpedo plane. Reconnoiter route Barcelona-Valencia. If nothing found, launch attack on seaplane carrier 'Daedalos' lying damaged in the port of Sagunto. Next: Radio-telegraphic order (FT). Make torpedo attack ojn vessels in the Valencia inlet. Execution: Aircraft 530.- 1 torpedo F 5..../...*

Order sent to aircraft by FT, attack on 'Daedalos' cancelled..../...

Attack 21:50 h. One torpedo from altitude of 20 m. 1,500 m. from target, against 'darkened' ship (lights out). Depth: 20 m. Torpedo dropped without incident. Angle: 90°. Aircraft speed: 130 km/h. Cross wind in direction of torpedo. Force 1-2. Depth of torpedo (3m.). Time to target: 1 minute and 35 seconds. Column of water, impact amidships. Wake clearly observed in searchlight beam. Ship sank slowly. The aircraft that attacked Valencia at 03:00 hours confirmed sinking. Defense consisted of 9 searchlights, Flak and AA machine-guns..../... Landing: 23:40 h. Duration of flight: 4 h. 40 min. Torpedoed ship: British 'Thorpeness' (7.400 Ldt. TRB), carrying food supplies."

The Republican official war report of 22 June confirmed the sinking: "*Aviation.- Continuing their aggressions against the cities in our rearguard, the foreign aviation in the service of the fascists made fresh attacks in the early hours of yesterday and today at Alcira, Barcelona, and Valencia. As a consequence of these aggressions against Valencia, the British ship 'Thorpheness' was sunk and the French merchant ship 'Somnion'* seriously damaged."

The sinking was attributed to the He 59 of the then *Hauptmann* Martin Harlinghausen, commander of AS./88 at that time and later creator of the *Luftwaffe's* first units of torpedo planes, which formed part of KG 26 and were equipped with Heinkel He 111 Hs and Junkers Ju 88 As. After numerous failed attempts, this had been the second successful use of a torpedo by the German pilots operating in the Spanish civil war since the end of the first world war (the first ship sunk was the *Edith* on 13.08.37). In 1971 Harlinghausen, then a Lieutenant General in the new *Luftwaffe*, attended a reunion of seaplane veterans of AS./88 with his former comrades Golcher and Brey, which was held in Ciudadela (Menorca).

Six months before, on 20 January 1938, the *Thorpeness* had been attacked by the Italians as she was moored in the port of Tarragona. At 08:20 h that day, three Savoia Marchetti SM. 79s of the Italian Legionary Air Force dropped twenty-five bombs, some of which exploded near the starboard side of the ship and causing around twenty casualties, ten of which were fatalities (seven crew members and three port workers). The attack had

A company of Spanish marines at the memorial service for four of the dead sailors from the "Thorpeness," killed six months earlier in the bombing attack carried out by aircraft of the Italian Legionary Air Force on the port of Tarragona.

Prayer for the dead seamen of the "Thorpeness" at the cemetary in Tarragona.

important international repercussions, as it coincided with a visit by a delegation from the British Labour party to Catalonia presided by the MP, Mr. Dobbie. The next day four of the British seamen were buried, their coffins covered with the Union Flag. They were given military honors by a company of Marines and an Air Force band, as well as the band of the Army's Nº 15 Regiment, which played funeral marches. The funeral was attended by civil and military delegations and representatives of political parties and unions, as well as Labor MPs, members of the local British ex-patriot community, and a large crowd, which silently paid homage to the dead. The bodies of the other three crew members had fallen into the sea and were recovered at a later date. The *Thorpeness*, once repaired, continued to make voyages between ports in England and the Spanish Republic until it was finally sunk on 21 June 1938.

During the return flight to Pollensa in the early hours of 21 June, Harlinghausen's Heinkel He 59 number 530 had also spotted the British merchant ship *African Trader* heading east, and he ordered the ship to Palma for inspection by use of the plane's searchlight, as it was not displaying the agreed identification signal. The following morning, following the British admiral's protests at the ship being diverted, the vessel was escorted to Valencia by the Royal Navy destroyer *Imogene*, and then to Gibraltar to verify its cargo.

The Heinkel He 59s of AS./88 were a nightmare for Republican maritime traffic.

The 3,045 ton British merchant ship *Sunion* (ex *Admiral Hasting*) was built in 1919 by William Gray & Co. Ltd. of West Hartlepool (England) for M.A. Embiricos Andros. It was later bought by African & Continental S.S. Co. of London, which in 1938 decided to begin transporting war materiel, acquiring five ships in total. One of these was the *Sunion* that, after making a voyage to the Bosphorus, and another from Oran to Cartagena, made another trip carrying war supplies from Oran to Alicante. The vessel was attacked three times consecutively and sunk by AS./88 in the early hours of 22 June while she was anchored just outside the port of Valencia with a cargo of Russian munitions, trucks, and cereals.

The British merchant ship "African Trader."

The British vessel "Sunion" sunk in the port of Valencia.

According to the AS./88 secret weekly report of 20 to 26 June 1938 sent by Harlinghausen to Berlin, the *Sunion* was attacked three times in the early hours of the 22 June.

The first took place at 03:00 hours and was carried out by Heinkel He 59 number 538, which dropped two 250 kg bombs from a height of sixty metres, with a gap of twenty-five metres. The first bomb struck the ship in front of the bridge and the second two or three metres next to the port side of the bow.

Seaplanes of AS./88 at their Pollensa base.

During the second attack made by the same seaplane, a 250 kg bomb, dropped from an altitude of seventy metres, fell two or three metres from the centre of the ship. However, there was no fire. There were defensive actions with searchlights and anti-aircraft fire.

The third attack came at 04:20 hours, this time by Heinkel He 59 number 531, which glided in from the SW at 3,000 metres. Flying at eighty metres, the seaplane dropped four 250 kg bombs and twenty incendiaries at twenty metre intervals, obtaining four hits in the cargo holds to the fore and aft and creating a huge fire and several explosions amidships. The plane encountered defenses consisting of anti-aircraft batteries, searchlights, and machine guns which began ten minutes before the attack and contiued during the same. According to intercepted Republican radio messages the ship sank later that day. At the end of the war it was found to be so badly dameged that no attempt was made to refloat it.

The AS./88 operational diary for 23 June contains an entry on both sinkings:

"*Note: The sunken ships mentioned in the report for 22 June were:*

a).- The British ship 'Thorpeness', 7,400 tons, carrying provisions.

b).- The British ship 'Sunion', 5,100 tons, carrying munitions, trucks and wheat."

Meanwhile, at 14:20 hours, also on the 22nd, Heinkel He 59 number 531 dropped two 250 kg bombs at an interval of fifteen metres from a height of eighty metres on a sailing vessel 1 km from the entrance to the port of Sagunto. One bomb fell in the water and the other hit the target, causing a large explosion with flames rising 150 metres, probably due to the fuel the ship was transporting. The vessel quickly sank. The anti-aircraft defenses from Sagunto were active.

Impressive sequence of photographs showing the attack on a sailing vessel near the port of Sagunto. In this first photo it is possible to see the 250 kg bombs dropped by the Heinkel He 59 falling in the water.

In the second, another 250 kg bomb hits the target.

In the third picture the vessel can be seen exploding, causing a 150 metre-high flame, which suggests the ship was carrying fuel.

Aerial view of the Columbretes Isles, located off the coast of Castellón.

On 25 June a *Kette* (flight) of three Heinkel He 59s (numbers 531, 535, and 536) of AS./88, each carrying twenty 50 kg bombs, received the order to support the cruisers *Canarias* and *Almirante Cervera* and two destroyers of the Nationalist fleet during the landing on the Columbretes Islands, located off the coast of Castellon, which were to serve as a valuable observation post in order to watch the maritime supply of Valencia. The objective of the operation was to capture the garrison and destroy the radio station, but not occupy the islands themselves, in the face of a possible Republican raid to retake them.

At 15:30 hours the planes flew in formation over the Columbretes Islands, first at 500 metres and later at a lower altitude.

A 50 kg bomb was dropped *(o.V.*, or *ohne Verspätung*, meaning without delayed fuse) on Puerto Tofiño and they began strafing with their 20 mm cannons. A man appeared near the lighthouse waving a white flag. The leading seaplane landed and three of the crew disembarked in a dinghy armed with pistols and a MG to find the island had been abandoned, with the exception of one man, that being the lighthouse keeper.

The naval forces arrived soon after and the *Canarias* sent a landing party ashore. As soon as the island had been secured and the flag raised at 17:40 the *Kette* took off for the return flight.

The month of June 1938 was one of the busiest and most successful for AS./88 during the Spanish Civil War, resulting in the loss of twelve merchant ships of different nationalities.

Magnificent photograph showing the nose of a Heinkel He 59.

7

The Blockade During the Second Half of 1938. Main Air Operations and War Service of AS./88

July

At 21:55 hours on 4 July a single Heinkel He 59 had been forced to land at sea due to a problem in its right-hand engine some fifteen miles east of the mouth of the river Ebro. At 05:55 hours on 5 July the seaplane was picked up and towed to base by the launch *Pollensa*.

On 7 July, three new twin-engined Heinkel He 59s arrived in the Balearic Islands from Italy, and were assigned to AS./88 as replacements for machines that had been lost.

The report of the German Naval Mission in Palma for 10 July signed by *Kapitänleutnant* K.W. Plaas notes the operations carried out by AS./ 88 on the night of 9/10 July.

Rear view of the right-hand engine gondola of a Heinkel He 59.

The report describes how three Heinkel He 59s had made a night sortie against the railway station in Benifayo and the station and war factory in Algemesí, where they caused an enormous fire.

The report goes on to add that: "*Continuing from the report for the night of 8 to 9 July it is very probable that a night fighter was brought down at 23:30 hours between Valencia and Alcira, by one of our aircraft*." This was a Polikarpov I-15 "Chato." The Republican fighter had reported the combat with the Heinkel He 59 that night, and report nº 285 of the D.E.C.A. in Valencia, dated 10 July, records that their fighter had taken off to intercept the seaplane, "*engaging the enemy aircraft with no visible result*."

Above: A Republican Polikarpov I-15 "Chato," which were frequently sent up to intercept the seaplanes. Below: A Heinkel He 59 of AS./88, paradoxically flying the pennant of the Non-intervention committee.

The Spanish freighter "Betis," which was bombed by AS./ 88.

Damage caused to a Heinkel He 59 by Republican anti-aircraft artillery.

The veteran 1,011 ton Spanish cargo ship *Betis* was built in 1879 by A. Leslie & Co. in Newcastle (England). The ship was owned by Jose Morey of Barcelona. The vessel was east of Vilanova and la Geltru, on the beach at Calafell, where it had run aground as it steamed close to the coast on its way from Torrevieja with a shipment of salt for Barcelona.

On 11 July, the tug *Montcabre* and the coastgaurd vessel *V-17 Juan Lucena* left the port of Barcelona to assist the *Betis*. During the night of 11/12 July both vessels were attacked twice by two Heinkel He 59s, with the *V-17 Juan Lucena* being hit, leaving three men wounded and causing varying degrees of damage. Both seaplanes were hit by anti-aircraft fire (Russian K-21 45 mm anti-aircraft cannon) from the stern of the coastgaurd ship.

The report issued on 12 July by the German Naval Mission in Palma includes the actions of AS./88 for the night of 11/12 July, recording among other things the attacks on the *Betis*. The first was carried out at 23:45 hours, although without hitting the target. The second, at 04:10 hours on 12 July, was when the ship was bombed and strafed by another Heinkel He 59, dropping a total of twenty 50 kg bombs, two of which hit the stern. Both seaplanes were damaged by gunfire.

Reoport N° 287 from the High Command of the Information Section of the D.E.C.A. in Barcelona, dated 12 July, confirmed the second attack:

"*At 04:55 an enemy seaplane appeared in the sky near Barcelona later heading for Tarragona. As it arrived at Calafell it turned over the ship 'Betis' aground near the coast. Once above the ship the aircraft dropped eight bombs* (sic), *and then strafed the vessel. Two bombs hit the stern, destroying the rudder. This aggression left three men with minor wounds*." At the end of the war the remains of the ship were scrapped "in situ."

A twin-engined Heinkel He 59 in the bay of Pollensa.

The 844 ton Danish merchant ship *Bodil* (ex *Matilda*) was built in 1922 by N.W. Werf of Zeeland (Holland) and, like the *Edith*, belonged to J. Lauritzen of Copenhagen. The ship was sunk at 17:00 hours on 21 July by Heinkel He 59 number 534, which dropped two 500 kg bombs from a height of fifty metres along with a score of incendiaries as the ship was underway some twenty-five miles southeast of Palamos. The *Bodil* had come from Gdynia and was carrying aircraft to the French port of La Nouvelle. Both 500 kg bombs hit the cargo hold. The ship turned onto its port side and sank. Prior to being sunk and after firing at the bridge, the seaplane signalled the crew with a heliograph to board the lifeboats and abandon ship. They were later picked up by the Royal Navy cruiser *Shropshire*. Enemy fighters made an attempt at defense but without success.

The Spanish cargo ship *Vicente* (ex *Vinaroz*, ex *Paris*) of 534 tons was built in 1899 by W. Harkess & S, Middlesbrough (England), and was owned by Vicente Ferrer Peset S.A. of Valencia. At 21:25 on 24 July it was sunk by a Heinkel He 59, which dropped four 250 kg bombs on the ship as it was attacking the port of Gandía, which had a mine-like effect and also damaged the British ship *Dellwyn*. The *Vicente* was refloated by the Naval Commission for Salvaging ships on 20 December 1939.

Above: The Spanish cargo ship "Vicente" was sunk in the port of Gandía.

Mechanics and armorers attach the last of four 250 kg bombs to a PVC 505 on a Heinkel He 59.

Report N° 301 of the High Command of the Information Section of the D.E.C.A. in Valencia, dated 25 July, confirmed events, stating: "*Last night at 22:35 hours, an enemy seaplane appeared over Gandia from the east. The aircraft attacked the port, dropping approximately fifteen 50 kg bombs and several incendiaries from a height of 2,500 metres. One of the explosions caused by the bombs resulted in the sinking of the 'Vicente'. Fortunately there were no casualties. The enemy plane disappeared from where it came.*"

25 July 1938: Beginning of the battle of the Ebro

That same day the Condor Legion's liaison officer received the following telegram for the commander of the unit:

"*Request that the Condor Legion element in the Balearic Islands participates in operations in the area of the river Ebro attacking road and rail networks tonight from Mora la Nueva to Tarragona.*"

The same day the Spanish motor-sailing vessel *Antonio Matutes* of 66 tons, owned by Antonio Matutes of Ibiza, was sunk at 04:00 by a Heinkel He 59 that dropped two 500 kg bombs from a height of one hundred metres as it lay in the port of Gandía. One of the bombs scored a direct hit, pulverising the vessel. When divers went down to look for the remains of the ship at a depth of six metres in November they only found the remains of the engine.

Report N° 301 from the D.E.C.A. in Valencia, dated 25 July, recognized the sinking, stating that: "*Gandia suffered another bombing attack today at 05:03 hours. Another seaplane coming from the east flew over the port at low altitude, dropping five 100 kg bombs* (sic) *and five incendiaries. One of these fell a metre from the British merchant ship 'Dellwyn' without exploding. Another caused the sinking of the packet 'Matute'. The rest of the bombs fell harmlessly on land. Four of the incendiaries dropped by the seaplane fell on the aforementioned British ship, which was also hit by shrapnel from some of the other bombs, although without consequences. The seaplane then left heading back east.*"

The Spanish motor-sailing vessel "Antonio Matutes" sunk at Gandía.

Unusual photograph of a pair of Heinkel He 59s, both fitted with the Rheinmetall Lb. 201de 20 mm cannon.

The 1,452 ton *Dellwyn* (ex *Madge Llewellyn*) was built in 1920 by J. Lewis & Sons Ltd., Aberdeen (Scotland), and belonged to Dillwyn S.S. & Co and was registered in Swansea. The ship had managed to break the blockade on five occasions with the help of British warships, entering the port of Bilbao. When the northern front disappeared she began trading with Republican ports in the Mediterranean. At the beginning of March she made a voyage from Oran to Valencia carrying war materiel, then Oran to Alicante with a cargo of coal in the middle of July.

At 20:50 hours on 26 July she was sunk by a Heinkel He 59, which dropped two 500 kg delayed fuse bombs on her from a height of eighty metres while she was moored in Gandia port. She was refloated on 10 May 1939 and towed to Valencia to be rebuilt. In

The British merchant ship "Dellwyn" was sunk in the port of Gandía.

Above: The port of Gandía, where the damaged "Dellwyn" can be seen on the right; behind it is the sunken "Antonio Matutes," and in the background is the "Vicente," damaged by bombs dropped by Heinkel He 59s. Below: Republican soldier of the *Defensa Especial Contra Aeronaves* (Special Defence Against Aircraft) unit, more commonly known as D.E.C.A.

March 1941 she was back in service with the name *Castillo Montesa*, being passed on to the Elcano National Company in July 1943. In 1959 she changed owners, and in 1961 became the *Aline*. She was scrapped in 1971.

Report Nº 303 of the D.E.C.A. in Valencia, dated 27 July, confirmed her sinking: "*A seaplane appeared over Gandía at 21:46 yesterday, and dropped two 500 kg bombs on the port and another of 100 kg* (sic), *which failed to explode. As a result of this aggression the British ship 'Dellwyn' was sunk and a house destroyed. Fortunately there were no casualties.*"

August

Major Harlinghausen, with the Iron Cross, in a photograph taken during the Second World War.

Hauptmann Martín Harlinghausen was promoted to *Major* and stayed on in Pollensa as commander (*Kommandeur*) of *Seefliegerstaffel* AS/88.

The report of the German Naval Misión in Palma dated 2 August included a note on operations carried out by AS./88 on 1 August, stating: "*21:15 h-21:50 h. 3 aircraft 40x50 and 4x250 kg bombs and incendiaries, from 150-200 m altitude on factory Paitrosa* (sic). *Target hit, large fire. Enemy responded with automatic weapons. 2 planes damaged by impacts, one forced to land at sea, crew rescued, one man wounded.*"

In effect, after bombing the factory at Paitrosos one of the Heinkel He 59s was forced to make an emergency landing at sea near San Carlos de la Rápita in order to attend to the wounds of the pilot, *Feldwebel/ Flugzeugführer* Herbert Euen. Soon after the crew were picked up by a torpedo launch. Everything indicates the plane was abandoned and did not return to service.

From 14:00 to 19:30 hours on 5 August, maritime reconnaissance was carried out along the route Barcelona-Marsaille. Enemy defensive measures consisted of fighters. The Heinkel He 59s repelled the attacks, hitting a Republican seaplane that had broken down and was taking refuge on the French coast.

On the night of 6 August the 2,120 ton British merchant ship *Lake Lugano*, built in 1900 and the property of Charles Strubin & Co, London, was attacked by a Heinkel He 59, which dropped four 250 kg bombs from a height of one hundred metres that fell close to the side of the ship as she lay in the port of Palamos. At 01:45, 01:55, and 02:35 hours during the morning of 7 August, three Heinkel He 59s dropped sixty 50 kg bombs and a number of incendiaries from an altitude of 50/100 metres on the ship as it was unloading cork, as well as the nearby port sheds, hitting their targets. On the ship, after several large explosions, a fire started which spread to the material being unloaded onto the dock.

The British merchant ship "Lake Lugano," bombed and set on fire in Palamós.

Ground crew of AS./88 preparing a Heinkel He 59 for its next mission.

The Spanish tanker "Campomanes," sunk in the port of Valencia.

The Spanish tanker *Campomanes* (6,276 tons) was built in 1932 by the *Sociedad Española de Construccion Naval* at its shipyards in Cadiz and belonged to the *Compañía Arrendataria del Monopolio de Petróleos S.A.* (C.A.M.P.S.A.). The ship was sunk at 21:45 on 15 August by a Heinkel He 59 that dropped four 250 kg bombs on the vessel from an altitude of one hundred metres as she lay moored in the port of Valencia. Three of the bombs hit the ship, exploding at the stern. The enemy anti-aircraft defenses consisted of searchlights and artillery. The *Campomanes* was refloated on 10 October 1938. On 26 December 1942 she was hit by torpedos on her port side as she made her way along the Portuguese coast between Cape Silleiro and Montedor, with an eight metre hole being ripped in her hull. In spite of the damage she was towed to El Ferrol.

At 02:20 hours on 19 August a Heinkel He 59, following a reconnaissance patrol in the Gulf of Rosas and near the coast of Cabo San Sebastián, dropped four 250 kg bombs from seventy metres on the coastguard vessel *V-10 Ana*, which was escorting the British merchant ship *Seabank Spray* from Vallcarca to Port de la Selva. One of the bombs hit the Republican vessel in the stern, killing three men and wounding others, as well as causing serious damage. The merchant ship was untouched. The patrol ship's anti-aircraft defenses responded to the attack with its 20mm Oerlikon cannon and 7mm Vickers machine gun.

View of the four PVC 505s used to carry four SC 250 (250 kg) bombs on the Heinkel He 59.

On 28 August an He 59 was lost in an accident following a night raid; this was aircraft number 532, piloted by *Unteroffizier* Harro Prengemann. The seaplane had landed in rough seas near Pollensa and was destroyed. Three of the crew were unhurt and *Unteroffizier* Walter Bulling was slightly hurt, while *Leutnant/Beobachter* Peter Römisch was seriously injured, with fractures in the lower third of one leg, which resulted in the amputation of a foot.

Series of photographs showing the recovery of the remains of Heinkel He 59 number 532 after its crash landing in the bay of Pollensa.The first photo shows part of the fuselage and a float. Below: In the second, an engine is brought to the surface.

In the third, the crane leaves a tangled mass of wood and steel tubes on the ground.

In the fourth photograph it is possible to see a part of the fuselage, which has remained reasonably intact.

September

On 10 September the only Heinkel He 60 then in service with AS./88 was permanently removed from operations due to an excess of flying hours and awaited its return to Germany.

On 16 September at 20:10 three Heinkel He 59s dropped sixty 50 kg bombs and a number of incendiaries from 100/200 metres on the aerodromes of Canudas and El Prat de Llobregat, near Barcelona. Many of the bombs hit aircraft and warehouses. Two planes were seen burning.

The nose of a Heinkel He 60 from AS./88 on which is painted the Squadron's "Ace of Spades" emblem.

The Republican aerodromes of Canudas and El Prat de Llobregat were repeatedly bombed by Heinkel He 59s of AS./88.

Four days later a Heinkel He 59 dropped four 250 kg bombs from a height of one hundred metres on a ship underway near Cabo Palos (Cartagena), with the bombs falling very close to the target. At 05:50 another Heinkel He 59 dropped twenty 50 kg bombs and several incendiaries on the aerodrome at San Javier, striking the hangars and fuel tanks and causing a series of explosions and fires.

According to the report of the Balearic Regional Air Command dated the 23rd, a patrol from the 2nd Unit (AS./88) bombed the industrial area of Alcoy (Alicante), while another patrol of Heinkel He 59s bombed the Bay of Mahon, with one of the aircraft being hit by shrapnel from the anti-aircraft artillery, but without serious consequences.

Above: San Javier aerodrome following a bombing attack by planes of AS./88. Below: Damage caused by a Republican anti-aircraft gun to the float of a Heinkel He 59.

At 20:20 hours on 29 September, a Heinkel He 59 dropped four 250 kg and five 50 kg bombs and a number of incendiaries on the port of Barcelona. Because of the low cloud and serchlights the crew were unable to assess the damage. On its return trip to base the seaplane spotted a suspicious merchant ship heading for Catalonia, which it forced to turn about and steer for Pollensa. This was a British ship that, once its cargo had been inspected, was allowed to continue.

October

According to the AS./88 operations report for 3 October sent by the German Naval Mission in Palma and signed by *Korvetten Kapitän* Gerfried Brutzer, from 19:20 until 02:10 on 2/3 October a patrol composed of five Heinkel He 59s made five attacks on the port of Barcelona, dropping a total of eight 250 kg and sixty 50 kg bombs, plus a number of incendiaries, which hit sheds on the docks and two British ships, the *Lake Geneve* and the *African Mariner*. One of the seaplanes was chased by four Republican night-fighters. There was heavy anti-aircraft fire and searchlights.

The official report of the Republican Ministry of Defense dated 4 October describes the events as follows: "*Aviation.- During last night and the early hours of today, foreign aircraft carried out five attacks on the port of Barcelona. One of the bombs damaged the British merchant ship 'Lake Geneve', wounding one of the crew. Another hit the 'African Mariner', another British vessel. All the aggressions were carried out by German Heinkels.*"

The following day at 00:30 four Heinkel He 59s dropped 57 sacks of bread rolls and propaganda on the city of Barcelona.

Patrol of Heinkel He 59s of AS./88 displaying the emblems of the Non-intervention Committee painted on their fuselage.

Devastating effect of the bombing of the port of Barcelona carried out by five Heinkel He 59s of AS./88.

6 October 1938: Farewell for the International Brigades in Barcelona

As evening fell on 8 October a Heinkel He 59 dropped six bombs on the station at the important railway hub at San Vicente de Calders (Tarragona), the bombs falling close to a passenger train travelling from Reus to Barcelona, which had stopped at the platform, with shrapnel hitting the first four carriages. Thirty people were killed and more than one hundred were wounded. This attack was the most costly in terms of human life as a direct result of an operation by AS/88, and rather strangely, the Republican official war report for that day did not record the number of victims, only mentioning the following:

"*Just after 20:00 hours today a foreign seaplane bombed San Vicente de Calders*."

Up until that date AS./88 had only bombed military targets with great precision and without causing civilian deaths, compared to other air units operating in the skies above Spain. Undoubtedly, it was this raid, together with the one on Denia (18.10.38) and the armaments factory at Carcagente (02.11.38), which will be examined later, which resulted in the largest massacres perpetrated by Heinkel He 59s of AS./88 during the Spanoish Civil War.

Four days later, on the 12th at 17:00 hours, the Junkers Ju 52/3m (W) was moored next to the cruiser *Canarias*, forty miles south of Formentera, to receive operations orders from the Nationalist fleet.

During the morning of 15 October several Heinkel He 59s bombed the port of Barcelona on three occasions and another attacked the aerodrome at Canudas, with one aircraft returning to Pollensa with combat damage. During this time the Squadron also again bombed the aerodrome at San Javier and a Republican patrol vessel off the coast of Cartagena, encountering heavy anti-aircraft fire and enemy CC&F Grumman G-23 "Delfín" fighters, although none of the seaplanes were shot down.

The port of Denia (Alicante) was attacked twice in the middle of October. First at 02:15 on 17 October by a single Heinkel He 59 from AS./88, which bombed the port, destroying five houses but without causing casualties. The second, more serious attack, was at 10:45 on 18 October, when three Heinkel He 59s dropped forty 50 kg and four 250 kg bombs, together with a number of incendiaries, from an altitude of 100/500 metres on sheds and the wharf in the port of Denia. The bombs hit their targets and caused large explosions and twelve casualties.

Above: A Heinkel He 59 upper-wing damaged by anti-aircraft fire. Below: The Grumman GE-23 "Delfíns" of the Republican nº 28 Group took part in the defense of the Cartagena naval base.

Effect of the bombing of Denia by AS./ 88. Above: The hand grenade factory was completely destroyed. Center: Burned sheds at the port. Below: One of the German 50 kg bombs that failed to explode.

The official Republican war report dated 19 October confirmed the attack, stating that: "*At 11:35 hours yesterday (18th), three Italian seaplanes* (sic) *bombed Denia killing 11 and wounding a further 52 people among the civilian population.*" Other sources claim there were 12 killed and 18 wounded, all of them military personnel who were working in a hand grenade store.

On 18 October a patrol of three Heinkel He 59s was attacked by three Grumman CC&F G-23 "Delfíns" as they reconnoitered the coast of Cartagena, although without consequences.

Ten days later, on the 28th, three Heinkel He 59s carried out reconnaissance fifteen miles north of Cabo Formentor, looking for the Cant Z-506 (73-1) of Lieutenant Colonel Ramon Franco, hero of the flight of the Dornier *Wal* "Plus Ultra" and at that time chief of the Balearic Regional Air Command. Two days later, two Heinkel He 59s carried out seven reconnaissance sorties each in an attempt to find him. Due to bad weather it was not until the 30 October that the remains of the seaplane and the bodies of four of the five crew were found.

Lieutenant Colonel Ramon Franco, killed in an air accident.

November

Republican sources assured that a Heinkel He 59 of AS./88 was shot down by Polikarpov I-15 "Chato" night-fighters on 2 November near Santa Cristina de Haro. However, in reality the plane managed to return to base with one crewman slightly wounded.

The Republican Polikarpov I-15 "Chato" fighters attacked the Heinkel He 59s on numerous occasions.

According to the AS./88 operations diary dated 3 November:

"*At 19:10 hours on 2nd November 1938, a single Heinkel He 59 dropped ten 50 kg bombs and several incendiaries from a height of 1,000 metres on a war factory in Carcagente (Valencia), hitting the target, causing thirteen casualties and destroying a dozen houses.*"

The Republican official war report for 3 November recorded the attack as follows:

"*The foreign aircraft also attacked Carcagente, causing the destruction of 12 dwellings and killing 13 and wounding another 15 of the local civilian population.*"

The Cypriot ship *Eleni* (ex *Wireless*, ex *Quillebeuf*, ex *Vernier*), 1,138 tons, was built in 1921 by Chantiers & Ateliers Ang Normand in Le Havre (France). The vessel belonged to Inter Levant S.S.Co Ltd Cyprus. The vessel made a trip from Marsailles to Barcelona carrying a suspicious cargo in September. According to the AS./88 operations diary for 5 November, she was attacked by four Heinkel He 59s throughout 4 November on a total of four occasions while moored in Águilas (Murcia) on route from Almeria with a shipment of grapes and explosives. The first two attacks were carried out from low altitude at 03:35 h and 20:00 h but were unsuccessful, as the bombs either fell in the sea or failed to explode. On the third and fourth attempts at 20:30 h and 21:00 h some of the 250 kg bombs and incendiaries found their target, causing explosions and fire on the bridge and in the hold of the ship, which began sinking on its side, leaning against the pier. She was refloated in February 1940 by the Naval Commission for Salvaging ships and then towed to Valencia for repair. On 12 April that year she was handed over to the Administration and renamed *Castillo Vera*. She then served with the Elcano National Company until 1947, when she was sold to Astur-Galaica to transport coal. She was wrecked at Estaca de Bares on 15 February 1948.

The Cypriot vessel "Eleni," sunk in the port of Águilas.

At 02:05 on 7 November, the British ship *Margaret Rose* was sunk by a Heinkel He 59 that dropped twenty 50 kg bombs on her while she was moored in the port of Almeria, hitting several other vessels. In the AS./88 official report for 9 November there is an entry by *Kapitän Leutnant* Karl Knappe stating: "*According to a red source, as a consequence of the attack on Almeria of 7.11, the British ship 'Margaret Rose' and the dredger 'Almeria' were sunk and the British 'Yorkbrook' and two minesweepers were damaged.*" The last two mentioned were the Republican minesweepers *D-171* and *D-173*, which were left out of commission.

Above: The British ship "Margaret Rose" was sunk in the port of Almeria. Below: A Heinkel He 59 flying over La Cenia aerodrome at Tarragona, the Condor Legion's base during the last phase of the war.

The dredger "Almeria," sunk in the port of the same name.

At the same time that same day, the same Heinkel He 59 had sunk the dredger *Almeria* of 564 tons, which belonged to the port authority.

On 8 November at 19:30, a Heinkel He 59 dropped five 50 kg bombs on a Republican coastguard vessel northeast of Sagunto, hitting the target and first burning, then sinking the ship. The ship had retalliated against the seaplane with small calibre amti-aircraft fire and the aircraft received several impacts.

In the early hours of 12/13 November, a flight of Heinkel He 59s bombed the port of Valencia, hitting the sheds along the docks, the Gomez workshops, and the C.A.M.P.S.A. installations, where they caused a large fire. The seaplanes were attacked by three Republican night-fighters, shooting one down for sure and another probable. One of the seaplanes returned with bullet holes.

Damage to the fuselage of a Heinkel He 59.

According to a dispatch from the 2nd Unit (AS./88) sent to the Balearic Regional Air Command at 15:30 hours on the afternoon of 15 November, two Heinkel He 59s again attacked the port of Denia. Both aircraft were hit by anti-aircraft fire. One of the planes was forced to make an emergency landing at sea in the area of Cabo San Antonio, in quadrant 2405, being towed back to base by the Squadron launch. The crew were unhurt.

17 November 1938: End of the battle of the Ebro

Above: A patrol of AS/88 Heinkel He 59s flying the pennants of the International Committee for Non-intervention. Below: The remains of a CAMPSA fuel tank in Valencia following bombing by AS./ 88.

An Oerlikon 20 mm anti-aircraft cannon belonging to the Republic's DECA.

Heinkel He 59 of AS./ 88 being towed by a launch.

December

On 4 December 1938 the 2nd unit—another designation for AS./88—was composed of eight operational Heinkel He 59s and one Junkers Ju 52/ 3m (See) with floats.

On 15 December, the Special Anti-Aircraft Defense (D.E.C.A.) in Barcelona hit a Heinkel He 59, seriously wounding the pilot, *Leutnant* Friedrich-Wilhelm Fritsch, who, with great effort, managed to return to Pollensa, saving both his aircraft and crew, although he himself was to die some hours later of diphtheria in the Palma de Mallorca military hospital.

On 18 December four more He 59s arrived in Pollensa to substitute another four planes that were undergoing repairs. At this time there were ten Heinkel He 59s operational and two undergoing repairs, as well as the Junkers Ju 52/ 3m (W) with floats operational and a Heinkel He 60 being repaired.

23 December 1938: The beginning of the Catalonian campaign

On 31 December five Heinkel He 59s, each carrying twenty 50 kg bombs, attacked the rail and road systems around Tarragona, Valls, Reus, and Cambrils. All targets were hit, although twenty bombs failed to explode. Targets destroyed in the raid included a train and four trucks. There were searchlights and anti-aircraft guns of different calibres in Reus and Tarragona. Heinkel He 59 number 538 did not return. The following day it was confirmed as

A Heinkel He 59 undergoing repairs.

Lieutenant José Falcó with his Polikarpov I-15 "Chato" of the night-fighter squadron.

having been shot down by a fighter over Valls and all its crew were killed (*Leutnant* (pilot) Otto Schmidt, *Oberleutnant* Karl-Friedrich Printz, *Reg. Inspekteur* Ludwig Müller, and *Unteroffiziers* Paul Jeck and Walter Bulling). The destruction of the He 59 was attributed to Jose Falco Sanmartin, commander of the Barcelona night patrol.

During 1938, under the command of *Major* Harlinghausen, AS./88 made a total of around six hundred sorties.

AVIACIÓN
NEGRILLOS

8

The End of the War. Main Air Operations and War Service of AS./88 During the First Three Months of 1939

January

It was during this month that the Squadron changed its commander again for what was to be the last time. *Major* Martin Harlinghausen returned to Germany and was relieved by *Hauptmann* Helmer Smit, who became the fifth and final commander of AS./88 from January to 1 April 1939, when the Spanish civil war ended.

In the early hours of 1 January, a Heinkel He 59 of AS./88 began to accumulate a large amount of ice on its wings, which caused it to spin and crash into the sea, killing the entire crew: *Leutnant zur See* Ernst Poeschel, *Leutnant* Schöbel, *Funk-meister* Zervas, and *Feldewel* Hereld. A total of six "Zapatones" spent the day searching for thc lost seaplane without success and the search was called off by nightfall.

Opposite: Flag bearer of the "*Aviación Negrillos*," which was the official name in Spanish for the different air units in the Condor Legion, at a table in the officers mess at Pollensa. Above: a Condor Legion commander decorating Smit, the last officer to command AS./88.

At 07:35 hours on 5 January a Heinkel He 59 dropped twenty 50 kg bombs from a height of three hundred metres, striking a ship in the port of Gandia, with some of the bombs falling on the wharf. Two Heinkel He 59s which that day had carried out a reconnaissance flight over the Barcelona-Tarragona-Gandia sector were attacked by enemy Polikarpov I-15 "Chato" fighters. One of the Heinkel He 59s was seriously damaged and was probably written off.

Above: A Polikarpov I-15 "Chato" of the Republican night-fighter squadron refuelling. Below: Damage inflicted on a Heinkel He 59 by an enemy fighter.

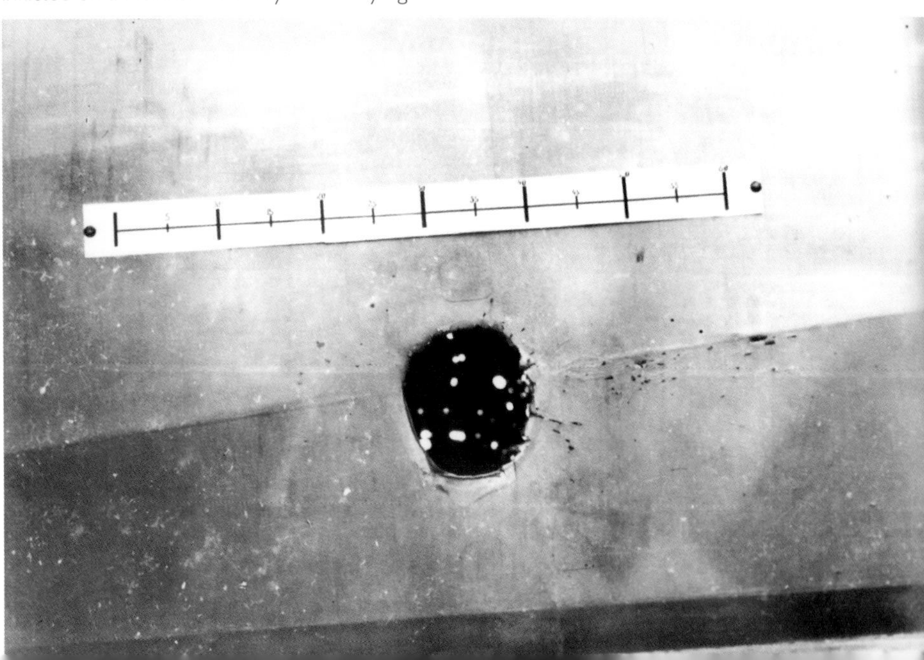

The following day at 19:00 hours a Heinkel He 59 dropped fifteen 50 kg bombs and various incendiaries from 1,000 metres on the port of Gandia, hitting several sheds and warehouses on the wharf. To the north of Gandia, the seaplane came under fire from the machine guns mounted on two Republican Russian-made Type G-5 torpedo boats, numbered 11 and 21. The vessel marked 11 was left aground on a beach near Cullera.

Above: A German mechanic holding the cable of a Heinkel He 59 in an almost comic pose. Below: Republican torpedo boat N° 11. Of Russian origin, this Type G-5 was run aground near Cullera after being attacked by a Heinkel He 59.

February

At 17:20 hours on 8 February, a Heinkel He 59 dropped twenty 50 kg bombs from 1,000 metres on the ports of Rosas and La Selva, hitting their targets and sinking a small sailing ship in La Selva. The vessel in question could have been the *Cala Pi*.

8 February 1939: The capitualation of Menorca

At 22:50 hours the same day, a Heinkel He 59 crewed by Germans of AS./88 took off from Pollensa for Menorca with Spanish Major Federico Noreña and Second Lieutenant Juan Apalategui aboard. At 00:30 hours on the 9th the plane landed in the port of Ciudadela, where the two Spanish officers disembarked in a rubber dinghy. In the Military Headquarters, Major Noreña took command of the Nationalist forces in Menorca.

At 16:50 hours on 9 February a Heinkel He 59 left Ciudadela for Pollensa carrying Captain Thomas and Second Lieutenant Apalategui, landing at the base in Pollensa without incident.

13 February 1939: End of the Catalonian campaign

March

At 07:50 hours on 6 March, a Heinkel He 59 made a forced landing at sea near Cabo de Palos (Cartagena) after being hit in the engine by a Republican Polikarpov I-15 "Chato." The Nationalist cruiser *Canarias* rescued the crew and sank the seaplane, as it could not salvage the aircraft.

Republican Polikarpov I-15 "Chatos" of the 2nd Flight of n° 26 Group managed to bring down a Heinkel He 59 on 6 March 1939, near Cartagena.

Above: Photographs showing the failed attempt to recover a Heinkel He 59 by the cruiser "Canarias" off the coast of Cartagena. In the first picture, the seaplane can be seen sinking on its starboard side, with both floats underwater. Below: In the second picture it is sinking on its port side.

The same day the 2nd unit of the Balearic Air Force was formed by the following seaplanes of AS./88: eight operational Heinkel He 59s; two Heinkel He 59s undergoing repairs; and one operational Junkers Ju 52/3m (W) fitted with floats.

On 7 March the Heinkel He 60 of the 2nd unit (AS./88) was transferred to the 1st unit (Nationalist Air Force) and numbered 60-5. This was to make up for a previous loss, and on 14 March a new Heinkel He 60 was made operational with the 2nd unit (AS./88).

Above: The third picture again shows the view from starboard. Below: The fourth picture shows the rescued crew of the He 59 aboard the "Canarias."

A Heinkel He 60 of AS./ 88 hanging on the crane at Pollensa.

Another Heinkel He 59 was accidently lost on 22 March twenty miles northwest of Ibiza, near the Isle of Es Vedrá, when it was forced to make an emergency landing due to engine problems. The crew were rescued by a Royal Navy destroyer and taken to Pollensa. On the same day the Republicans claimed that a Heinkel He 59 had been shot down by one of their CC&F Grumman G-23 "Delfín" near Cartagena, although this was denied by the Nationalists. However, it is very probable that the aircraft was no longer operational with AS./88.

Finally, on 26 March 1939 two more Heinkel He 115 A-0 torpedo planes were made operational with the 2nd unit. At that time the unit was composed of ten Heinkel He 59s, a Junkers Ju 52/3m (W), and a Heinkel He 60, as well as the two recently incorporated Heinkel He 115s.

The He 115s had flown in from Marienehe, via Friedrichshafen and Italy, with the civil registration numbers D-ANTP and D-AOHS. In Pollensa, under the supervision of the Heinkel engineer Dr. Gerhard Geike, they were evaluated by technicians from the Staff of the Nationalist Air Force for possible purchase, carrying out perhaps three or four reconnaissance flights. Other sources, based on the Heinkel archives, claim that the objective was not to promote the aircraft in Spain, but rather to test the effects of corrosion in the Mediterranean sea.

The aircraft were completely painted in a grey-green color (RLM 02). The civil numbers were erased, and they were painted with a St Andrews cross in black and white, as well as the precept black rosettes on the sides of the fuselage and wings, but they were not given a Spanish number.

German Heinkel He 115 seaplane with the black rosettes recently painted on its fuselage.

Another view of a Heinkel He 115 at Pollensa.

Dr. Geike had arrived in Pollensa aboard one of the Heinkel He 115s, together with the *Bordmechaniker* Burmeister and Dortmund, the *Bordfunker* Schröeder, *Leutnant zur See* Jandrey, *Leutnant* Wacksmuth, and other personnel, both air and ground, all of whom were members of the *Luftwaffe*. The two aircraft returned to Germany in May, and upon examination it was found that both aircraft had suffered serious structural damage in the metal parts due to the effects of corrosion.

1 April 1939: The End of the Spanish Civil War

German mechanics working on a Heinkel He 115.

Despite the poor quality of the photograph, it is possible to see two Heinkel He 59s together with two Heinkel He 115s recently arrived from Germany.

9

Spanish Airmen in AS./88

From October 1938 several pilots from the Spanish 2 G-62/73 Group were attached to the German seaplane unit at Pollensa (Mallorca). On the 15th of that month the following personnel arrived at AS./88, these were: the pilots Captain Luis Lerdo de Tejada Baylleres, the Lieutenants Celestino Ramos Serantes and Pedro Humbertum, and Second Lieutenant Dino Landini; two observers, Lieutenants Melchor Sangro Torres and Justo Fernández Fernández-Trapa; two radio operators, Sargeant Andrés Julve Izquierdo and Corporal Jaime Morro Llabrés; as well as four mechanics, Second Lieutenants Alberto Fadón Pérez and Jacinto Guillén Nanclares, Sargeant Francisco García, and Corporal Javier Rifá Mas.

A little later they were joined by pilot Captain Carlos Pombo Somoza, who had been appointed commander of the Spanish personnel attached to AS./88. He was accompanied by the Lieutenants—pilot and observer respectively—José Cortón Díez and José Romero Ruiz. The radio operators Sargeant Juan Manuel Nuño Ortiz and Corporal Enrique Robledo González were also sent. However, Captain Lerdo de Tejada and Lieutenant Sangro left after being transferred to other posts. Lieutenant Sangro was later killed in a Cant Z-506 along with Lieutenant-Colonel Ramón Franco.

Opposite: Captain Carlos Pombo Somoza. Left: Lieutenant Celestino Ramos Serantes. Right: Lieutenant Melchor Sangro Torres.

Above: Lieutenant Justo Fernández Fernández-Trapa. Below: A group of Spanish airmen attached to AS./ 88 at Pollensa.

Spanish airmen Manuel Alcalá and Justo Fernández playing chess in the officers mess at Pollensa.

On the left, with the bicycle, is Celestino Ramos, and on the right is Manuel Alcalá.

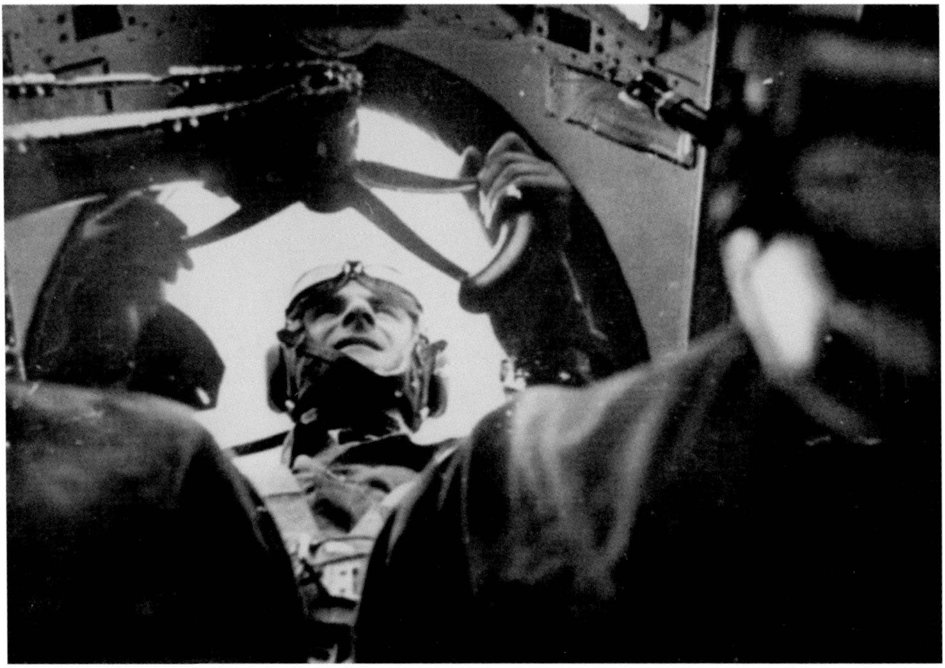

Carlos Pombo at the controls of a Heinkel He 59.

A beached Heinkel He 59.

The Spanish crews flew between October 1938 and March 1939 in the following thirteen Heinkel He 59s, according to their flight records: 528, 531, 534, 536, 537, 539, 540, 541, 542, 543, 544, 545, and 546.

The most outstanding actions involving the Spanish crews aboard the He 59s were the operations carried out in the taking of Menorca, the details of which fall outside the objectives of this study.

At the end of hostilities only three twin-engined Heinkel He 59s were handed over to the Spanish, the remainder being sent back to Germany.

A Babcock & Wilcox crane at the base at Pollensa winching a Dornier Wal (70-16) belonging to the Nationalist Air Force.

Spectacular photograph showing the damage caused to the "English Tanker" in the port of Alicante.

10

Conclusions

There was a *Luftwaffe* report made after the Spanish Civil War which concluded by saying that the air operations carried out by AS./88 against Republican surface vessels had been of little or limited success.

It remains unknown as to how and why this conclusion was reached, but what is certain is that of the 148 ships which were either captured or sunk by the Nationalists during the conflict, forty-eight of these were by the seaplanes of AS./88, twenty-six by the Nationalist Airforce and the Italian Legion, eight by the Condor Legion, and the rest by surface units or submarines of the Nationalist Fleet.

The higher rate of success scored by the seaplanes of AS./88 compared to the other air units could be explained as being due to an advantage of having naval pilots or personnel with specific air-sea training. The result of this was that a total of 27 Heinkel He 59s employed by AS./88 (between four to twelve at any given time) carried out 850 sorties and were responsible for forty-eight enemy vessels captured or sunk (approximately 100,000 tons) during the period the campaign lasted; that is to say, 32 % of the total.

The mail ship "Delfín."

The Republican destroyer "Almirante Antequera."

The Republican cruiser "Libertad."

The Spanish Civil War was the scenario in which German naval pilots were able to gain combat experience, above all in the first launching of torpedos from the air against surface vessels since the end of the First World War. Twelve such attacks were carried out, resulting in the following:

30.1.37 The mail ship *Delfín*. The torpedo failed to detonate.
31.01.37 The steamship *Nuria Ramos*. The attack was aborted under orders.
25.04.37 The main body of the Republican Fleet before Motril. One torpedo launched but again failed.
06.05.37 The Republican cruiser *Libertad*. The torpedo passed close to the stern.
09.06.37 The Republican destroyer *Almirante Antequera*. Close miss.
20.07.37 3 He 59s armed with torpedos tasked to attack ships in Valencia. Mission aborted.
12.08.37 Danish Merchantman *Edith*. Prior to bombong a torpedo was launched but failed.
13.08.37 Danish merchantman *Edith*. Another torpedo launched, this time with success and the ship sunk.
07.09.37 A Republican squadron involved in combat at Cherchel. One torpedo launched and failed.
09.10.37 British steamship *Cervantes*. Torpedo launched which the ship was able to avoid.
21.06.38 The seaplane carrier *Dedalo*. Order to attack cancelled at the last moment.
21.06.38 British steamship *Thorpeness*, torpedoed and sunk at Valencia.

The Squadron also developed the tactic of shuting off their engines and silently gliding over the target at low altitude (25 /100 metres) during night bombing attacks, surprising both the enemy anti-aircraft artillery and fighters. The great risks run during these missions gave good results but, as has been seen, the cost was high, both in human lives (17) as well as aircraft (17?).

The seaplane carrier "Dedalo."

He. 59.

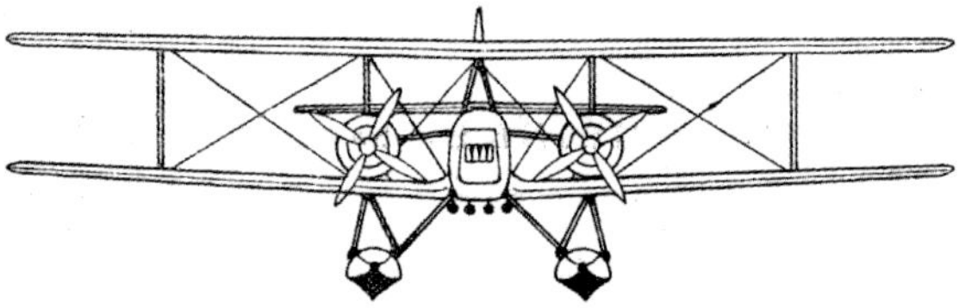

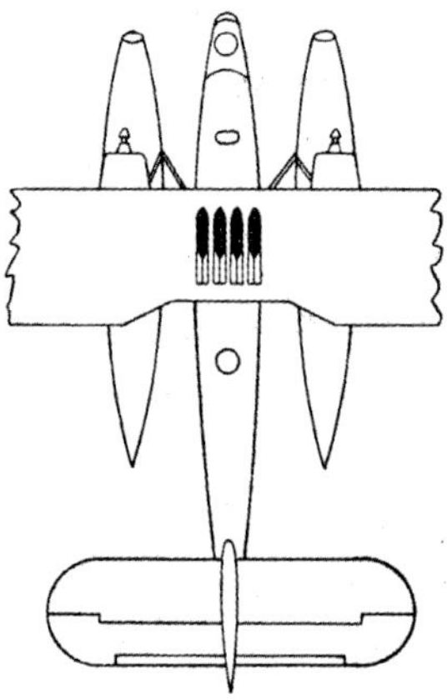

4 bombas de 250 K N - Disposit. de lanzamiento 4 lanzabombas: P.V.C. 505.

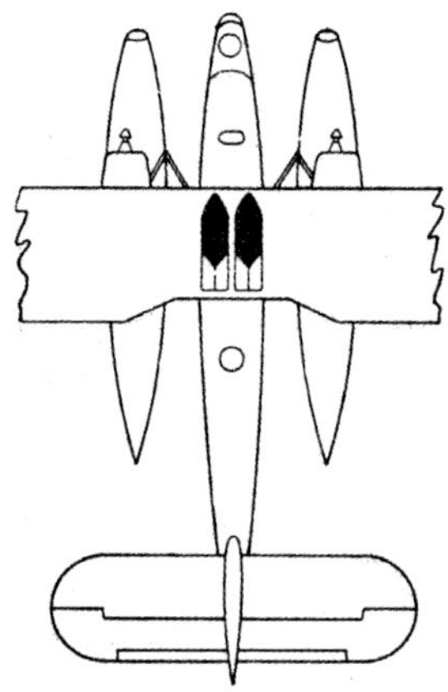

2 bombas de 500 K N Dispositivo de lanzamiento 2 lanzabombar P.V.C. 505

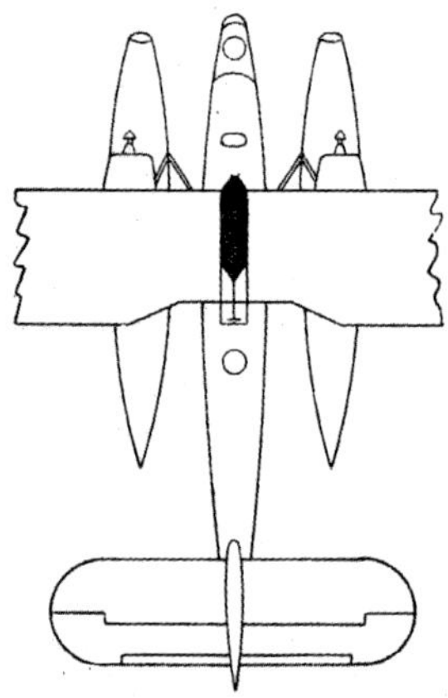

1 torpedo de 700 a 1000 K N Dispositivo de lanzamiento 1 lanzatorpedo 1005 P.V.C

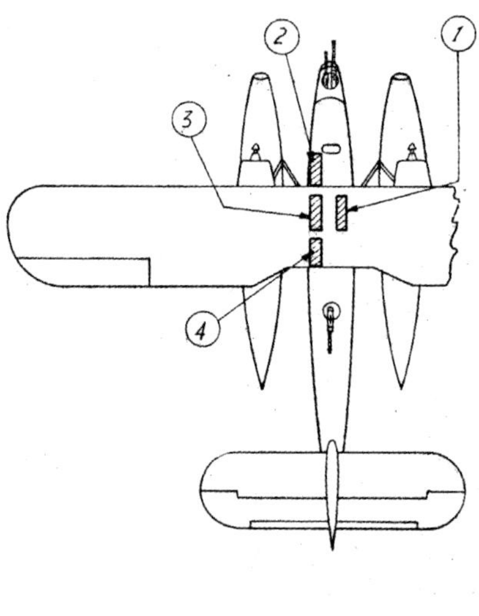

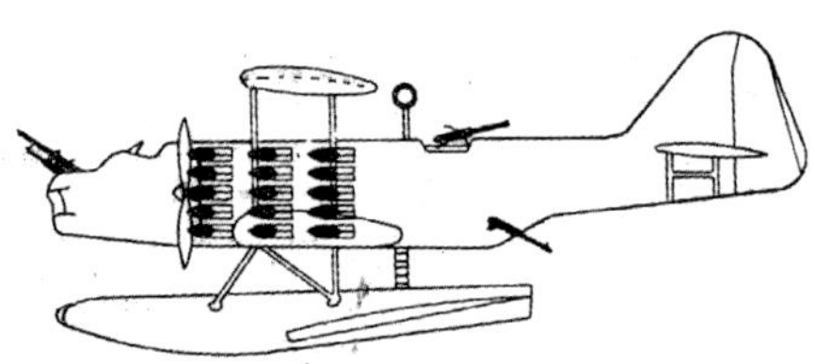

20 bombas de 50 K N - Dispositivo de lanzamiento 4 lanzabombas MAGA - 5 - C 50

Las cajas portabombas, marcadas con los números 1 y 3, son desmontables, pudiéndose montar en su lugar, dos depósitos auxiliares de gasolina

ARMAMENTO DEFENSIVO

3 ametralladoras de torreta M G-15 calibre 7'92 m m situadas en la siguiente forma: Una en la torreta de proa, con 13 tambores de 75 disparos.- Una en la superior posterior, con 13 tambores de 75 disparos - Una en la inferior posterior, con 9 tambores de 75 disparos, en total 35 tambores con 2,625 disparos En la torreta de proa, lleva tambien un cañon, tipo "LB 201" calibre 20 m.m. con 10 tambores cargadores de 20 disparos, en total 200 disparos.

Appendix I:
The Aircraft

HEINKEL HE 59 (nicknamed "Zapatones" or "Eiserne Gustav")

Country: Germany.
Manufacturer: Ernst Heinkel Flugzeug Werke G.m.b.H.
Type: Twin-engined biplane fitted with floats and central fuselage designed for day and night bombing, torpedo, and long range reconnaissance missions during the Spanish Civil War.
Engine: Two BMW VI U 12 cylinder engines, with water or Ethyl-Glycol cooling system, engine 60° V with six cylinders each side. The BMW model VI engine was built indistinctly with or without a propeller differential and used a system of cogs with the Farman compensated tooth mechanism. The engine functioned with two different compression ratios: e = 6 and e = 7:3. Both engines were mounted in gondolas supported on the lower wing.
Power: A) Engines with e=7:3 compression ratio: 750 hp. At normal cruising speed: 520/560 hp.
B) Engines with e= 6 compression ratio: 690 hp. At normal cruising speed: 520/550 hp.
Propeller: Four-bade wooden propeller, fixed speed of 3.84 m in diameter.
Structure: Steel tubes and wood, covered with canvas. The front of the fuselage was armored, except the glass nose and the windows in the rear turret.
Dimensions: Wing span: 23.80 m; Length: 17.40 m; Height: 7.17 m; Wing surface: 153.20 m^2.
Weight: Dry: 5,000 kg; In flight: 9,100 kg; Lift capacity: 4,100 kg; Weight/Power ratio: 6.82 kg/hp.
Performance: Maximum speed at sea level: 210 km/h.
Cruising speed: 170 km/h at 1,440 rpm.
Landing speed: 120 km/h.
Rate of climb: 225m/minute.
1,000 m.: 4 minutes and 18 seconds.
2,000 m.: 11 minutes and 12 seconds.
4,000 m.: 26 minutes.
Ceiling: 7,000 metres.
Operational Range: 470 km without auxiliary tanks (5.5 hours); 765 km with auxiliary tanks (9 hours).
Take off distance: 350 m.
Fuel tanks: Two: 850 litre tank in each float, either aluminium or rubber. Two 500-litre auxiliary tanks instead of boxes of 50 kg bombs. Total fuel: 1,700 litres without aux tanks and 2,700 with aux tanks.
Oil tanks: Two 70 litre aluminum tanks behind each engine.
Radio: Telefunken transmitter type En. G. 5; receiver type E. 4 A.

Crew: Four/five. Pilot and three crew members.
Offensive Armament: One 7.92mm Rheinmetall-Börsig MG-15 mounted in the nose turret, with 13 seventy-five round drums served by the observer. Many of the Heinkel He 59s in Spain replaced the MG with a Rheinmetall (ex Solothurn) Lb 201 Cal. 20 mm cannon with 10 twenty round drums/magazines. Very effective against ground and naval targets.
Defensive Armament: Two Rheinmetall-Börsig 7.92mm MG-15s located in turrets: one in the rear upper fuselage (dorsal) with 13 seventy-five round drums and another in the lower rear fuselage (ventral) with 9 seventy-five round drums. Both machine guns were operated by bombardier-gunners. Counting all three machine guns (offensive and defensive) there were a total of 35 drums containing 2,625 rounds.
Payload:
A) One *LT lufttorpedo* (air torpedo) Norwegian Horton type, made under licence in Kiel (Germany) by Schwartzkopf, designated LT F 5. Weight: 737 kg. Warhead: 200 kg. Length: 4.80 m. Diameter: 45 cm. Motor: Four cylinder radial – compressed air and alcohol. Range: 2,200 m. Speed: 33 knots. Launch speed: 75 knots from a height of between 15 to 25 m.
B) 1.000 kg of bombs of different types and combinations: 2 500kg SC 500 bombs. Launch mechanism: 2 external PVC 505 racks. 4 250kg SC 250s. Mechanism: 4 external PVC 505 racks. 20 50kg SC 50s. Mechanism: 4 internal MAGA 5 C 50 Vc in 4 bomb carrying boxes, 2 of them dismountable, allowing two auxiliary fuel tanks to be fixed to the aircraft.
Several 10kg SD 10 C Anti-personnel bombs and B1 incendiaries.

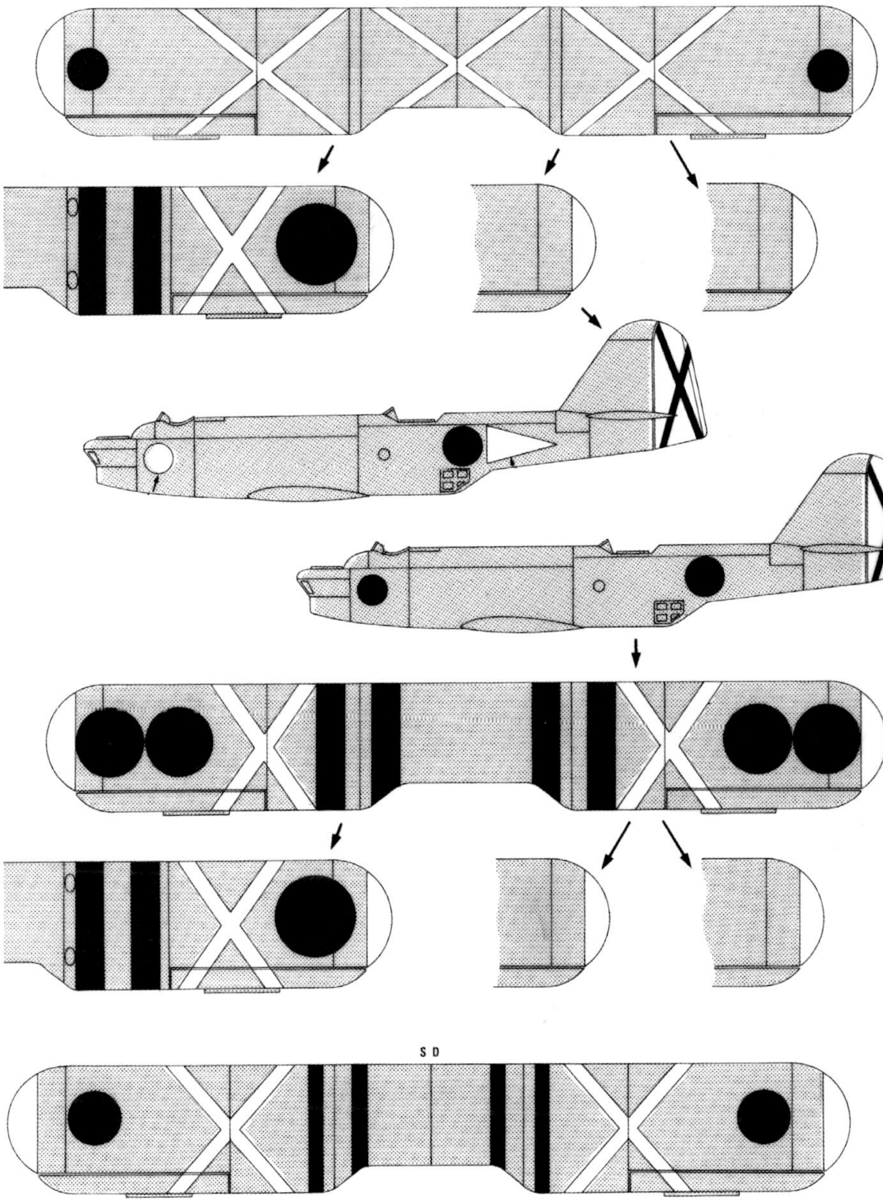
S D

He-60

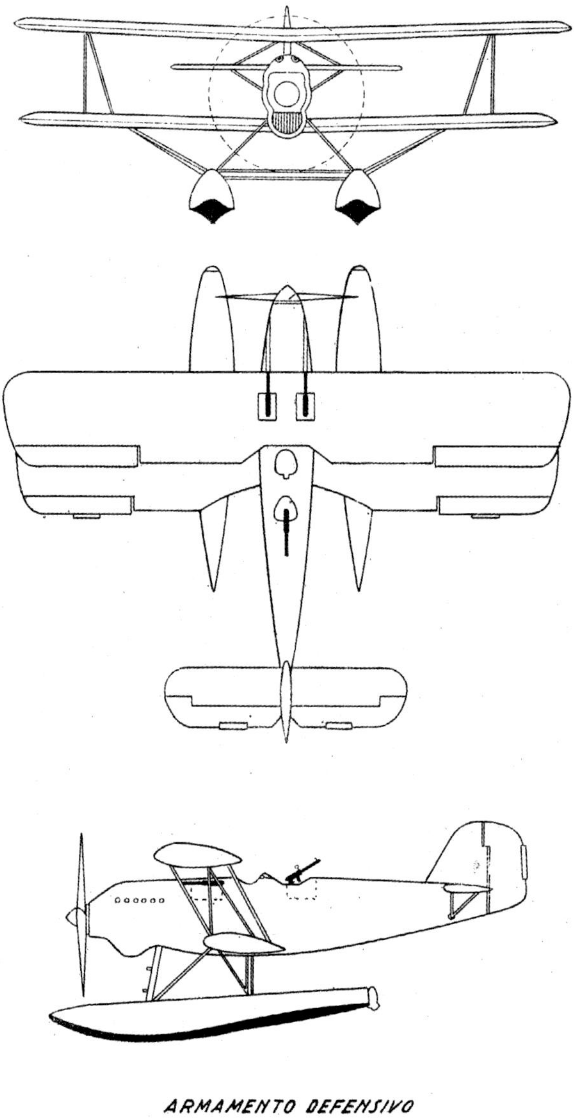

ARMAMENTO DEFENSIVO

2 ametralladoras de capot, sincronizadas M-G-17, calibre 7,92 con 1.000 disparos cada una. Su alimentación se efectua por cinta metálica articulada.
1 ametralladora de torreta, M-G-15, calibre 7,92, situada en la parte superior del fuselaje detrás del piloto, con 11 tambores de 75 disparos, en total 825 disparos. Dotación completa 2.825 disparos.

HEINKEL HE 60

Country: Germany.
Manufacturer: Ernst Heinkel Flugzeug Werke G.m.b.H.
Type: Single-engine biplane with floats and central fuselage, designed as a short range reconnaissance seaplane to be catapulted from German warships. Employed during the Spanish Civil War in coastal reconnaissance tasks and occasionally bombing.
Engine: Single BMW VI U, Series 8 V12 cylinder water-glycol cooled engine. Maximum power at take off 710 hp at 1,660 rpm and 556 hp at 1,523 rpm when cruising.
Propeller: One Schwarz two-blade wooden propeller, fixed speed and 4.02 m diameter, weighing 51.90 kg without axle casing.
Structure: Mixed construction, oval section fuselage of steel tubes and canvas, except the engine and 685 litre aluminium fuel tank. The two 2.20m wide wings were canvass covered wood. Two 7.80 m long floats made from lightweight metal.
Dimensions: Upper wing span: 13.50 m.; Lower wing span: 13.00 m.; Length: 11.55 m.; Height: 5.15 m.
Weight: Empty: 2,413 kg; In flight: 3,600 kg; Lift capacity: 1,187 kg; Weight/Power ratio: 5.14 kg/hp.
Performance: Maximum speed at sea level: 225 km/h.
Maximum speed at 2,000 m: 225 km/h.
Maximum cruising speed: 190 km/h.
Landing speed: 100 km/h.
Rate of climb: 5.45 m/second.
1,000 m.: 4 minutes.
4,000 m.: 20 minutes.
Ceiling: 6,000 m.
Operational Range: At maximum speed: 720 km; Cruising speed: 850 km (4.5 hours).
Take off distance: 300 m.
Fuel tank: One 685 litre aluminum tank.
Oil tank: One 60 litre aluminum tank.
Radio: Telefunken transmitter type Fug 5; receiver type E.4.
Crew: Two: pilot and observer.
Offensive Armament: Two synchronised fixed belt-fed 7.92mm MG-17s with 1,000 rounds each in the nose.
Defensive Armament: One turret mounted 7.2mm MG-15 located in the upper fuselage in a revolving turret in the observer's position, with 11 seventy-five round drums. A total of 2,825 rounds was carried for all three machine guns.
Payload: Two C-10 IX racks carrying six 10 kg bombs each.

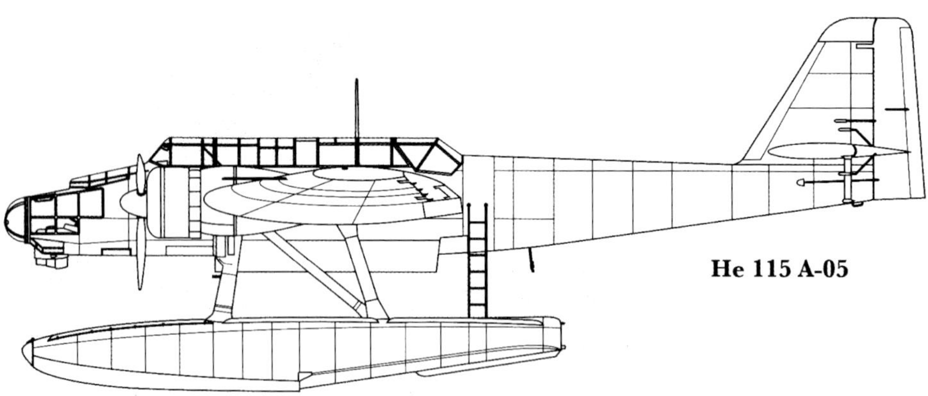

He 115 A-05

HEINKEL HE 115 A-O

Country: Germany.
Manufacturer: Ernst Heinkel A.G.
Type: Twin-engined monoplane with floats. Reconnaissance, torpedo, and bomber seaplane also used for anchoring magnetic mines during the Second World War.
Engine: Two BMW 132 K 960 hp 9 cylinder air-cooled radial engines.
Propeller: Two metal VDMs with three blades, 3.30 m diameter.
Structure: Monoplane, entirely metal construction, two-spar mono-hull fuselage. Two metal floats 10.20m in length.
Dimensions: Wingspan: 22.28 m.; Length: 17.30 m.; Height: 6.60 m.
Surface of aerodynamic lift: 86.70 m^2.
Weight: Empty: 5,410 kg; Loaded: 9,400 kg.
Performance: Maximum speed: 315 km/h at 3,400 m.
Cruising speed: 305 km/h.
Landing speed: 100-115 km/h.
Ceiling: 4,300 m.
Operational Range: 2,000 km.
Crew: Three: pilot, observer-bombardier, and radio-telegraphist.
Defensive Armament: One dorsal 7.62mm MG-15 served by the observer, mounted in the cockpit.
Payload: One torpedo or 1,250 kg of bombs.

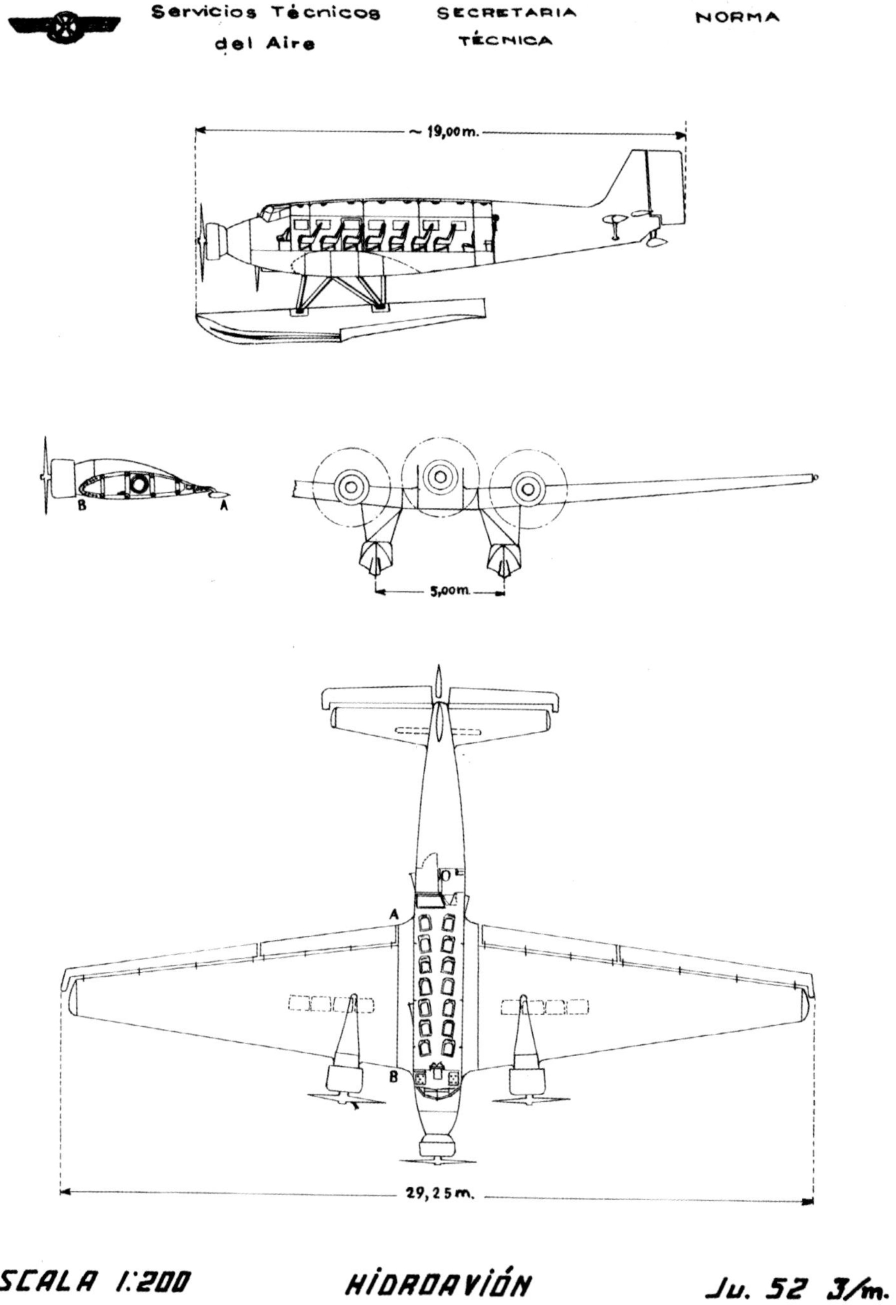
Servicios Técnicos
del Aire
SECRETARIA
TÉCNICA
NORMA
~ 19,00 m.
B
A
5,00 m.
A
B
29,25 m.
ESCALA 1:200
HIDROAVIÓN
Ju. 52 3/m.

JUNKERS JU 52/3m (W)

Country: Germany.
Manufacturer: Junkers.
Type: Tri-engined monoplane, used to transport personnel and carry out liaison tasks for AS/88 during the Spanish Civil War.
Engine: Three BMW 132 T 9 cylinder 830 hp air-cooled radial engines.
Propeller: Three two-blade metal propellers.
Structure: Metallic, and completely covered in undulating metal sheets; multi-spar wings with flaps and "double-wing" ailerons. Semi-monohull. Two metallic floats.
Dimensions: Wingspan: 29.21 m; Length: 18.99 m; Height: 5.41 m; Surface area: 110.50 m^2.
Weight: Unloaded: 7,110 kg; Total: 10,977 kg.
Performance: Maximum speed at sea level: 254 km/h.
Maximum speed 3,000 feet: 262 km/h.
Cruising speed at 3,000 feet: 207 km/h.
Rate of climb to 3,000 m: 19 minutes.
Ceiling: 5,053 m.
Operational Range: 1,500 km.
Crew: Five: pilot and co-pilot, observer-navigator, radio-operator, and bombardier-gunner.
Defensive Armament: Two dorsal machine guns, one 7.62mm MG-15 7.92mm calibre and a 13mm MG-131 located in the sides of the fuselage.

Appendix II: Personnel

Nº	Surname/Name	Rank	Arrived/Returned	Notes
1	Althof Walter	*Fw./Flgz.Sattl.*	13.08.38	
2	Andrae Robert	*Uffz./Flgz.Mech.*	01.04.38	
3	Anhäuser Wilhelm	*Uffz./Flgz.Mech.*	01.02.38	
4	Arendt Heinrich	*Uffz./Rechn.Fhr.*	16.07.38	
5	Auffermann Hans Jürgen	*Lt.z.S./Beob.*	01.11.38/Mar.1939	
6	Aurich Hans	*Fw./Bordmech.*	19.11.38	
7	Barella Rudolf	*Uffz./Flg.*	Jul.1937/Nov. 1937	
8	Bätzholdt Fritz	*Uffz./Beob.*	Mar.1939/Apr.1939	
9	Baumann Enrique	*Fw*		
10	Baumbusch Heinrich	*Uffz./Bordmech.*	23.11.38	
11	Beck Eugen	*Ogefr./Funk.*		4/Ln.88.
12	Becker Alfred	*Ogfr./Flgz.Mech.*	10.11.38	
13	Becker Georg	*Uffz./Beob.*	Feb.1937 Nov.1937	
14	Behrendsen Jürgen	*Ziv./Masch.*	21.09.38	
15	Beisiegel Guillermo	*Uffz.*		
16	Berthold Herbert	*Ogefr./Motorenschl.*	19.03.38	
17	Beuster Kurt	*Ogefr./Flgz.Mech.*	21.01.38	
18	Beuster Rufino	*Uffz.*		
19	Beyert Hans	*Fkm./Beob.*	Jul. 1937/Nov.1937	
20	Bialek Albin	*Uffz./Beob.*	Jul.1937/Nov.1937	
21	Bigalk Gerhard	*Lt.z.S./Beob.*	Jul.1937/Nov.1937	
22	Billing Alfred	*Uffz./Bootsstr.*	01.04.38	
23	Bischoff Enrique	*Uffz.*		
24	Böhme Karl	*Ziv./Obepr.*	22.06.38	
25	Borbe Matías	*Uffz.*		
26	Born Rudolf	*Gefr./Torp.Mech.*	06.08.38	
27	Börner Ernst	*Ogefr./Flgz.Klr.*	27.10.38	
28	Böse Heinz	*Ogefr./Flgz.Mech.*	10.11.38	
29	Bramel	*Fw.*		
30	Brammer Erwin	*Lt.z.S./Flg.*	Oct.1937/Mar.1938	
31	Bremme Heinz	*Uffz./Flg.*	Mar.1939/Apr.1939	
32	Brey Franz	*Lt./Beob.*	Feb.1938/Apr.1939	Individual Military Medal
33	Brundiers Hans	*Uff./Waffwt.*	30.06.38	
34	Brutzer Gerfried	*Korv.Kptn.*	24.08.38	German Naval Mission /Palma
35	Bülling Walter	*Uffz./Bordmech.*	30.07.38/(+)31.12.38	
36	Burkhardt Erich	*Ogefr./Flgz.Mech.*	19.03.38	
37	Burmeister	*Bordmech.*	Mar.1939 May.1939	

38	Calmberg Albert	*Lt.z.S./Beob.*	Feb.1937/Nov.1937	
39	Carstens Julius	*Uffz./Flgz.Tischl.*	13.08.38	
40	Clausen Carl	*Uffz./Bordmech.*	12.05.38	
41	Clauss Rudolf	*Uffz./Beob.*	Feb.1937/Jul.1937	
42	Cords Heinz	*Uffz./Flg.*	Mar.1939/Apr.1939	
43	Deecke Joachim	*Lt.z.S./Beob.*	Dec.1937/Jul.1938	Repatriated
44	Diester Ewald	*Fw.*		
45	Dieterischs Horst	*Lt.z.S./Beob.*	Feb.1939/Apr.1939	
46	Dietze Alfons	*Gefr./Funk.*		4/Ln.88
47	Dolla Bruno	*Gefr./Flgz.Elr.*	06.08.38	
48	Dortmund	*Bordmech.*	Mar.1939/May.1939	
49	Dostal Erich	*Ogefr,/Flgz.Satlr.*	06.08.38	
50	Düring Otto	*Uffz./Funk.*		4/Ln.88
51	Dumke Karl	*Uffz.*		
52	Dralle Alfred	*Fw.*		
53	Drechsler Helmuth	*Fw.*		
54	Dröse Walter	*Uffz./Bombt.*	08.12.37	
55	Eberhardt Wilhelm	*Uffz../Flgz.Mech.*	01.02.38/Mar.1938	
56	Edler Johann-Peter	*F.T.-Ing. Telefunken*	13.08.38	
57	Einhaus Hermann	*Uffz./Beob.*	Mar.1939/Apr.1939	
58	Eke Alfred	*Fw./Beob.*	Feb.1939/Apr.1939	
59	Ellermann Konrad	*Fk.Mstr./Beob.*	May.1938/Nov.1938	
60	Erdmann Albin	*Fw.*		
61	Ermert Pius	*Ogefr./Flgz.Mech.*	27.10.38	
62	Ernst Willi	*Ogefr./Flgz.Mech.*	27.10.38	
63	Euen Herbert	*Fw./Flg.*	11.05.38/Dec.1938	Wounded AA
64	Fehling Ludwig	*Lt./Flg.*	May.1938/Nov.1938	
65	Feuchter Ernst	*Uffz./Beob.*		
66	Fiehn Helmuth	*Lt.z.S./Beob.*	Mar.1939/Apr.1939	
67	Fisher Alfred	*Ofw./Flg.*	Feb.1937/Jul.1937	
68	Fischer Carlos	*Uffz.*		
69	Floraks Johannes	*Gefr./Funk.*		4/Ln.88
70	Fort Juan	*Fw.*		
71	Fuchs Erwin	*Fw.*		
72	Fürll Erich	*Ofw./Flg.*	02.07.38/Jan.1939	
73	Franz Gerhard	*Ofw./Flg.*	26.01.38/Dec.1938	
74	Fritsch Friedrich W.	*Lt.z.S./Beob.*	12.05.38/(+)15.12.38	
75	Gaessler Johann	*Ofw./Flg.*	Nov.1936/Jul.1937	
76	Garling Willi	*Uffz./Motorenw.*	25.03.38	
77	Gassau Carlos	*Fw.*		
78	Geike Gerhard	*Ing.*	Mar.1939/May.1939	
79	Gensior Ottomar	*Ogefr./H.Beob.*	30.07.38/Jan.1939	
80	Gerbig Walter	*Ofw./Flg.*	Jul.1937/Nov.1937	
81	Geyer Ewald	*Uffz./Instw.*	01.04.38	
82	Gölcher Heinz	*Oblt./Beob.*	Sep.1937/Mar.1938	
83	Götz Willi	*Ofw./Flg.*	Nov.1937/May.1938	
84	Greve Hans	*Uffz./H.Beob.*	09.11.38/Mar.1939	
85	Gries Eugen	*Fw./ Flg.*	Feb.1937/Jul. 1937	
86	Grimme Alfred	*Ogefr./Flgz.Mech.*	19.03.38	

87	Grützmacher Günther	*Lt./Beob.*	Feb.1938/Sep. 1938	
88	Günsel Fritz	*Ogefr./Motorenschl.*	21.04.38	
89	Günther Friedrich	*Ogfr./Flgz.Mech.*	01.04.38	
90	Häckel Fritz	*San./Uffz.*	11.08.38	
91	Hageman Josef	*Uffz./Fallsrw.*	24.02.38	
92	Hanel Werner	*Fk.Mstr./Funk.*	19.03.38	
93	Harlinghausen Martin	*Maj./Staffel-Kapt.*	Jan. 1938/Dec.1938	4th CO AS/88
94	Hass Bruno	*Uffz./Flgz.Mech.*	27.10.38	
95	Hauer Wilhelm	*Ogefr,/Bordmech.*	13.09.38	
96	Havenstein Klaus	*Oblt./Beob.*	27.08.38/Mar.1939	
97	Hefele Hans	*Hptm./Flg.*	Jul.1937/Jan.1938	3rd CO AS/88
98	Hegner Walter	*Uffz./Flg.*	Nov.1938/Mar.1939	
99	Heinrich Franz	*Uffz./Bordmech.*	13.09.38/Mar.1939	
100	Heinrich Rudolf	*Uffz./Bomwt.*	19.03.38	
101	Heisig Kurt	*Ogefr./Funk.*	01.04.38	
102	Henkel Wilhelm	*Ogefr./Funk.*	25.03.38	
103	Hennecken Karl	*Ogefr./Motorenschl.*	21.04.38	
104	Hensel Herbert	*Ogfr./Flgz.Mech.*	10.11.38	
105	Hereld	*Fw.*	May 1938/(+)01.01.39	
106	Hermann Hans	*Uffz./Fernsp. .*		4/Ln.88
107	Hermann Martin	*Reg.Rat.Dr./Ltr.d.Wewa*	W./88	
108	Hertel Martin	*Uffz./Funk.*	4/Ln.88	
109	Heyroth Gerhard	*Ogefr./Bildw.*	20.08.38	
110	Hildebrant Sigfrido	*Uffz.*		
111	Himmler Franz	*Uffz./Schr.*	12.03.38	
112	Hinrisch Ernst	*Uffz./Flg.*	13.09.38/Mar.1939	
113	Hinterberger Josef	*Fw./Beob.*	Nov.1937/May.1938	
114	Hinz Herbert	*Uffz./Motorenw.*	25.03.38	
115	Hochbaum Wolfgang	*Lt.z.S./Beob.*	Mar.1939/Apr.1939	
116	Hoffmann Germán	*Uffz.*		
117	Hoffmann Karl	*Uffz.*		
118	Hoffmann Kurt	*Ogefr./Funk.*	24.09.38	
119	Hoffmann Willi	*Gefr./Funk.*		4/ Ln.88
120	Hohlfeld Rudolf	*Ogefr./Funk.*	01.04.38	
121	Höltken Walter	*Ogefr./Funk.*		4/Ln.88
122	Holz Reinhard	*Gefr./Flgz.Mech.*	10.11.38	
123	Hopf Albin	*Ogefr./Torp.Mech.*	30.06.38	
124	Horst	*Lt.*		
125	Hörstke Kurt	*Lt.z.S./Beob*	Jan.1938/Aug.1938	
126	Hüth Karl	*Ogefr./Flgz.Mech.*	10.11.38	
127	Hütten Heinz	*Ogefr./Torp.Mech.*	08.04.38	
128	Iserloth Werner	*Uffz./Beob.*	Mar.1939/Apr.1939	
129	Jäckle Hans	*Ogefr./Flgz.Mech.*	19.03.38	
130	Jäger Karl	*Uffz./Weterragt.*		W/88
131	Jandrey Siegfried	*Lt.z.S./Beob.*	Mar.1939/Apr.1939	
132	Jannsen Jürgen	*Oblt./Beob.*	Jul.1937/Feb.1938	
133	Jeck Paul	*Uffz./H.Beob.*	13.09.38/(+) 31.12.38	
134	Jessen Heinrich	*Uffz./Rechn.Fhr.*	20.07.38	
135	Jeworowski Waldemar	*Ogefr./Bootshz.*	01.04.38	

136	Jonske Erich	*Stábsartz Dr./ Truppenartz*	14.08.37	
137	Jürgens Hayo	*Oblt./Beob.*	Sep.1937/(+) 21.03.38	
138	Kahl Harald	*Uffz./Flg.*	Nov.1937/(+) 13.01.38	
139	Kahl Walter	*Ogefr./Flgz.Mech.*	01.04.38	
140	Kaiser Ernst	*Ogefr./Flgz.Mech.*	01.04.38	
141	Kapteina Georg	*Ogefr./Flgz.Mech.*	10.11.38	
142	Karnecki Emil	*Fk.Mstr./Funk.*	16.07.38	
143	Kastius Bernd	*Uffz./ Funk.*		4/Ln.88
144	Keck Werner	*Hpt.Fw./Komp.-Feldw.*	12.03.38	
145	Keese Hans	*Lt.z.S./Beob*	Jul.1937/Feb.1938	
146	Keitzel Kurt	*Uffz./Beob.*	Feb.1938 (+) 21.03.38	
147	Kellner Hans	*Uffz./ Dolm.*	19.11.36	
148	Kettner Paul Hugo	*Oblt.z.S./Beob.*	Jan. 1939/Apr.1939	
149	Kirschner Jacob	*Uffz./Torp.-Mech.*	26.07.38	
150	Kleyenstüber Arno	*Uffz./Beob.*	Jul.1937/Jan.1938	
151	Klümper Werner	*Oblt./Beob.*	Nov.1936/Jul.1937	
152	Klünder Günther	*Hptm/Flg.*	Feb.1937/Jul.1937	2nd CO AS/88
153	Knappe Karl	*Kptn.Lt.*	Oct.1938	German Naval Mission/Palma
154	Köhl Helmut	*Uffz./Fernsp.*		4/Ln.88
155	Köplin Walter	*Uffz./Bordmech.*	13.09.38	
156	Kuss José	*Uffz.*		
157	Langanki Ernst	*Uffz./H.Beob*	12.05.38/Dec.1938	
158	Lange Alfred	*Uffz./Beob.*	Mar.1939 Apr.1939	
159	Lateit Gustav	*Uffz./Ges.Fhr.*	25.03.38	
160	Latislaus Fritz	*Ofw./Flg.*	May.1938/Nov.1938	
161	Lausen Heinrich	*Ogefr./Flgz.Mech.*	27.10.38	
162	Leckband August	*Uffz./Motorenpr.*	09.04.38	
163	Leicht Dieter	*Lt./Beob.*	Nov.1936/(+) 05.02.37	
164	Lellmann Werner	*Gefr./Flgz.Mech.*	10.11.38	
165	Linge Georg	*Uffz./Beob.*	May 1938/Nov.1938	
166	Lipfert Walter	*Obfkmt./Funk.*	01.04.38	
167	Logeman Heinz	*Uffz./Beob.*	Aug. 1937	
168	Lohmeyer Peter	*Oblt.z.S./Beob.*	13.09.38/Mar.1939	
169	Lohre Anton	*Uffz./Flgz.Mech.*	19.03.38	
170	Lorenz Emil	*Fkmt./Funk.*	25.03.38	
171	Lust Georg	*Fw./Flg.*	09.04.38/Nov.1938	
172	Mahl Otto	*Ofw./Flg.*	Jul.1937/Nov.1937	
173	May Adolf	*Uffz.*	25.03.38	
174	Mauderer	*Uffz./Bordmech.*		
175	Mayer Anton	*Uffz./Mont.*	19.10.38	
176	Meissner Rudolf	*Lt./Flg.* Jan.	1938 Aug.1938	
177	Merrettig Hans	*Gefr./Bomwt*	20.08.38	
178	Metzger Reinhard	*Lt.z.S./Beob.*	Mar.1939/Apr.1939	
179	Miosga Alfred	*Gefr./Funk.*		4/Ln.88
180	Mommertz Kurt	*Stbs.Fkg./Beob.*	Jul.1937/Nov.1937	
181	Müller Ernst	*Uffz./Bordmech.*	19.11.38	
182	Müller Hans	*Uffz./Bordmech.*	19.11.38	

183	Müller Guillermo	*Uffz.*		
184	Müller Georg	*Uffz./Bordmech.*	13.09.38	
185	Müller Johannes	*Fw./Obw.Mstr.*	09.02.38	
186	Müller Ludwig	*Reg.-Insp.*	(+) 31.12.38	
187	Müllers Josef	*Ogefr./Flg.Mech.*	10.11.38	
188	Neumann Federico	*Uffz.*		
189	Nickelsen Peter	*Uffz./Motorenschl.*	13.08.38	
190	Niemann Franz	*Ogfr./Kan.*	25.03.38	
191	Niesel Fritz	*Uffz./Funk.*		4/Ln.88
192	Niess Walter	*Fw./Flg.*	09.04.38	
193	Nitzsche Hans	*Uffz./Beob.*	Dec.1937/Jul.1938	
194	Orth Jorge	*Fw.*		
195	Otto Paul	*Uffz./Mont.*	19.10.38	
196	Ossowski Otto	*Uffz./Flg.*	Nov.1937/May.1938	
197	Papendieck Siegfried	*Gefr.*	(+) 09.04.37	
198	Parschau Werner	*Uffz./Flgz.Mech.*	27.10.38	
199	Pätzold Heinz	*Ogefr./Flgz.Mech.*	27.10.38	
200	Peter Manfred	*Fw./Beob.*	May.1938/Jan.1939	
201	Pieper Herbert	*Uffz.*		
202	Pisters Peter	*Ogefr./Flgz.Mech.*	27.10.38	
203	Plaas K.W.	*Kptn.Lt.*	Aug.1938	German Naval Mission/Palma
204	Podeyn Willi	*Ogefr./Bordmech.*	12.05.38	
205	Poeschel Ernst	*Lt.z.S./Beob.*	May.1938/(+) 01.01.39	
206	Pohlmann Ernst	*Uffz./Bomwt.*	20.07.38	
207	Prengemann Harro	*Uffz./Flg.*	May.1938/Dec.1938	
208	Priemer Josef	*Fw./Wkmstr.*	10.11.38	
209	Printz Carl-Friedrich	*Oblt./Beob.*	13.09.38/(+) 31.12.38	
210	Randorf Paul	*Uffz./Flg.*	Jan.1939/Abr.1939	
211	Rasquin Enrique	*Uffz.*		
212	Rathberger	*Ofw./Flg.*		
213	Ratmeyer Heinrich	*Gefr./Torp.Mech.*	20.08.38	
214	Reefe Hans	*Lt.z.S./ Beob.*	Aug.1937	
215	Reich Oscar	*Ziv.*		
216	Reichert Ernst	*Ogefr./Flgz.Mech.*	27.10.38	
217	Reimer Willi	*Ogefr./Motorenschl.*	01.04.38	
218	Reppchen Fritz	*Hptm.(E)/ Z.b.V.*	24.08.38	
219	Rheinhold Paul	*Ogefr./Waffwt.*	20.08.38	
220	Richter Hermann	*Ogefr./Funk.*	02.02.38	
221	Rieckmann Peter	*Uffz./Bordmech.*	13.09.38	
222	Riecker	*Uffz.*		
223	Römisch Peter	*Oblt./Beob.*	12.05.38	
224	Rücker Rudolf	*Ofw.*	Mar.1938/Dec.1938 POW	
225	Rudolph Helmuth	*Uffz./Beob.*	Feb.1939/Apr.1939	
226	Rüter Robert	*Ogefr./Funk.*	19.03.38	
227	Sack Erwin	*Ogefr./H.Beob.*	13.09.38	
228	Salcher	*Oblt./Flg.*	Feb.1938	
229	Salis Willi	*Fw./Waffwt*	01.02.38	
230	Schadow Willi	*Uffz./Bordmech.*	23.11.38	

231	Schallmayer Friedrich	*Lt./Beob.*	Feb.1937/Nov.1937	
232	Scharschmidt Helmuth	*Fw.*		
233	Schiller Walter	*Ost.-Fkg./Beob.*	Jul.1937/Nov.1937	
234	Schinze Heinz	*Obgfr./Beob.*	May.1938/Dec.1938	
235	Schlinder Heinrich	*Uffz./Beob.*	Jul.1937/Jan.1938	
236	Schlüter Robert	*Gfr./Funk.*		4/ Ln.88
237	Schmehl Gerhard	*Fw.*		
238	Schmidle Emil	*Uffz./Bordmech.*	16.07.38	
239	Schmidt Edwin	*Obfkgst.*		
240	Schmidt Otto	*Lt./Flg.*	13.09.38/(+) 31.12.38	
241	Schmidt Rudi	*Uffz./H.Beob.*	13.09.38/Mar.1939	
242	Schmidt Teo	*Fw.*		
243	Schmidt Wilhelm	*Ogefr./Motorenschl.*	21.04.38	
244	Schneider Herbert	*Lt.z.S./Beob.*	Feb.1939/Apr.1939	
245	Schöbel	*Lt.*	Aug.1938/(+) 01.01.39	
246	Schoenthier Ewaldo	*Uffz.*		
247	Schocker Heinz	*Uffz./Flg.*	Feb.1939/Apr.1939	
248	Scholing Friedrich	*Uffz./Bomwt.*	18.08.38	
249	Schrep Jonny	*Gefr./Fernsr.*		N.O.-M.Palma
250	Schröeder	*Bordfunk.*	Mar.1939/May.1939	
251	Schultz Priedhelm	*Uffz./Flg.*	Mar.1939/Apr.1939	
252	Schultzen Gustav	*F.Mstr./H.Beob.*	05.08.38	
253	Schulze Hans	*Uffz./Beob.*	Oct.1938/Apr.1939	
254	Schwandt Ferdinand	*Ofw./Flg.*	Jul.1937/Nov.1937	
255	Schwarze Herbert	*Ofw./Flg.*	Feb.1937/Jul.1937	
256	Schwencke Hans Viktor	*Lt./Flg.*	Mar.1939/Apr.1939	
257	Schwilden Horst	*Oblt./Flg.*	Jul.1937/Jan.1938	
258	Seiler Herbert	*Uffz.*		
259	Siepen Wilhelm	*Uffz./Beob.*	Jul.1937/Feb.1938	
260	Singer Josef	*Uffz./Mont.*	19.10.38	
261	Smidt Helmer	*Hptm./Beob.*	Jan.1939/Apr.1939 5th CO AS/88	
262	Söhngen Ludwig	*Ogefr./Flgz.Mech.*	10.11.38	
263	Solbach José	*Lt.*		
264	Spirka Willi	*Uffz./Beob.*	Mar.1939/Apr.1939	
265	Spörl Alfred	*H.Gefr./Fernsr.*		N.O.-M.Palma
266	Stachelhaus Ernst	*Ogefr./Flgz.Mech.*	01.04.38	
267	Steffen Robert	*Uffz./Flgz.Mech.*	02.03.38	
268	Steinhaus Adolf	*Uffz./Flgz.Mech.*	27.10.38	
269	Stier Federico	*Fw.*		
270	Stinshoff Erich	*San.-Uffz.*	01.04.38	
271	Stoodt Arthur	*Ofw./Flg.*	Nov.1937/May.1938	
272	Storp Siegmund	*Lt./Beob.*	Sep.1936/Jul.1937	Military Medal
273	Stötzer Bruno	*Ofw.*	Feb.1938/Dec.1938	POW
274	Strauch Jorge	*Korv.Kptn.*	Jan.1938/Jul.1938	German Naval Mission/Palma
275	Ströhmaier Hermann	*Ofw./Flg.*	Feb.1938/Dec.1938	POW
276	Teupen Heinrich	*Ogefr./Flgz.Mech.*	10.11.38	
277	Therhaag Wilhelm	*Ogefr./Flgz.Mech.*	01.04.38	
278	Thewalt Carl-Hugo	*Oblt./Beob.*	13.09.38	

279	Thiele Alfred	*Ogefr./Waffwt.*	16.07.38	
280	Thier Wilhelm	*Ogefr./Flgz.Mech.*	01.02.38	
281	Thomsen Ernst	*Lt.z.S./Beob.*	Jul.1937/Feb.1938	Repatriated
282	Toball Claus	*Lt.z.S./Beob.*	Mar.1939/Apr.1939	
283	Tonollo Alfred	*Ofw./Flg.*	Oct.1937/Dec.1938	POW
284	Troll Dietrich	*Oblt./Flg.*	Jan.1939/Apr.1939	
285	Verlohr Friedrich	*Oblt./Flg.*	Jul.1938/Jan.1939	
286	Vitinghoff	*Uffz.*		
287	Von Büllov Karl	*Lt./Beob.*	May.1938/Dec.1938	
288	Von Frankenberg Egbert	*Oblt./Flg.*	Nov.1938/Mar.1939	
289	Von Müller Ludwig	*Oblt./Beob*	27.08.38/Mar.1939	
290	Von Seggern Enrique	*Uffz.*		
291	Wacksmuth Kurt	*Lt./Flg.*	Mar.1939/Apr.1939	
292	Wagenführ Karl	*Uffz./Motorenschl.*	01.04.38	
293	Walk Eugen	*Fw./Flg.*	Sep.1938/Mar.1939	
294	Wehle Rudolf	*Ogefr./Waffwt.*	06.08.38	
295	Weimann Wilhelm	*Uffz./Motorenschl.*	19.03.38	
296	Wendler Kurt	*Uffz./Wetterfunk.*		W/88
297	Werner Gerhard	*Lt./Flg.*	Nov.1938/Mar.1939	
298	Werner Kurt	*Uffz.*	Jan.1938/(+) 21.03.38	
299	Wessels Bernhard	*Uffz./Beob.*	16.11.38/Mar.1939	
300	Westphal Frank	*Obfk.Mstr./H.-Beob.*	12.05.38/Dec.1938	
301	Winkler Leonhard	*Uffz./Bomw.*	01.02.38	
302	Winse Bernhardt	*Uffz./Flg.*	Nov.1936/Jul.1937	
303	Wirth Josef	*Uffz./H.Beob.*	12.11.38/Mar.1939	
304	Witthinrich Werner	*Uffz./Flgz.Tischl.*	21.04.38	
305	Woch Helmuth	*Ogefr./Beob.*	13.09.38/Mar.1939	
306	Wodtke Wolf	*Lt.z.S./Beob.*	07.09.38/Mar.1939	
307	Wolf Karl Heinz	*Hptm./Beob.*	Oct.1936/Feb.1937	1st CO AS/88
308	Wrede Otto	*Fk.Mstr./Beob.*	May.1938/Dec.1938	
309	Wunderlich Herbert	*Uffz./Bordmech.*	23.07.38	
310	Zennig Herbert	*Ziv./Dolm.*		4/Ln.88
311	Zenker Volkmann	*Lt./Flg.*	Oct.1937/May.1938	
312	Zervas	*Funk.*	Nov.1938/(+) 01.01.39	
313	Zischka Antonio			
314	Zum Broecke Otto	*Fw./Flg.*	Feb.1939/Apr.1939	
315	Zunker Karl	*Lt./Flg.*	Jan.1938/(+) 21.03.38	

Abbreviations

Beob..- Beobachter (Observer)
Bilw..- Bildwart (Photographer)
Bootshz..- Bootsheizer (Stoker)
Bootsstr..- Bootssteuerer (Helmsman)
Bomwt..- Bombenwart (Bombardier)
Bordfunk..- Bordfunker (Radio Operator)
Bordmech..- Bordmechaniker (Flight Engineer)
Dolm..- Dolmetscher (Interpreter)
Fallsrw..- Fallschirmwart (Parachute Packer)
Fernsp..- Fernsprecher (Telephonist)
Fernsr..- Fernschreiber (Teletypist)
Fk.Mstr..- Funkmeister (Master Radio Operator)
Flg..- Flieger (Airman)
Flgz.Elr..- Flugzeug.Elektriker (Aircraft Electrician)
Flgz.Fhr..- Flugzueugführer (Aircraft Commander, pilot)
Flgz.Klr..- Flugzeug.Klempner (Plumber)
Flgz.Mech..- Flugzeugmechaniker (Aircraft Mechanic)
Flgz.Satlr..- Flugzeug.Sattler (Aircraft Suttler)
Flgz.Tischl..- Flugzeug.Tischler (Carpenter)
Funk..- Funker (Radio-telegraphist)
Fw..- Feldwebel (Warrant Officer 2)
Gefr..- Gefreiter (PFC)
Ges.Fhr..- Geschützführer (Chief Armourer)
Hptfw..- Hpt.Feldwebel (Regimental Sargeant Major)
Hptm..- Hauptmann (Captain)
Insp..- Inspekteur (Inspector)
Instw..- Instrumentenwart (Instrument Specialist)
Kan..- Kanonier (Gunner)
Kptn..- Kapitän (Captain)
Kptn.Lt. Kapitän Leutnant (Lieutenant)
Korv.Kptn..- Korvetten Kapitän (Corvette Captain)
Lt..- Leutnant (2nd Lieutenant)
Lt.z.S. Leutnant zur See (Ensign)
Maj..- Major (Major)
Masch..- Maschinist (Machinist)
Mech..- Mechaniker (Mechanic)
Mont..- Monteur (Fitter)
Motorenpr..- Motorenprüfer (Engine Inspector)

Motorenw..- Motorenwärter (Engine Specialist)
Obw.Mstr..- Oberwerkmeister (Workshop Master)
Obfk.Mstr..- Oberfunkmeister (Master Radio Operator)
Oblt..- Oberleutnant (First Lieutenant)
Oblt.z.S..- Oberleutnant zur See (Ensign)
Oblslt..- Obersleutnant (Lieutenant Colonel)
Ofw..- Oberfeldwebel (Warrant Officer 1)
Ogefr..- Obergefreiter (Corporal)
Obpr..- Oberprüfer (Chief Engine Inspector)
Rechn.Fhr..- Rechnungsführer (Chief Accountant)
San..- Sanitair (Medic)
Schr..- Schreiber (Writer)
Staffel.Kpt..- Staffel.Kapitän (Flight Lieutenant)
Torp.Mech..- Torpedo.Mechaniker (Torpedo Mechanic)
Uffz..- Unteroffizier (Sargeant)
Waffw..- Waffenwart (Armourer)
Wk.Mstr..- Werkmeister (Workshop Master)
Wetteragt. Wetterangest. (Meteorologist)
Wetterfunk..- Wetterfunker (Radio Meteorologist)
Ziv..- Zivil (Civil Servant)

Appendix III: Losses in Personnel and Materiel

	Rank	Name/Surname	Date	Place	Observations
1	Uffz.	Walter Bulling	31.12.38	Valls	Shot down fighter (Falco)
2	Lt.	Friedrich W. Fritsch	15.12.38	Pollensa	Wounded AA Barcelona
3	Fw.	Hereld	01.01.39	At sea	Accident frozen wing
4	Uffz.	Paul Jeck	31.12.38	Valls	Shot down fighter (Falco)
5	Oblt.	Hajo Jürgens	21.03.38	Cambrils	Shot down fighter (Sarrio)
6	Uffz.	Harald Kahl	13.01.38	Pollensa	Drowned on landing
7	Uffz.	Kurt Keitzel	21.03.38	Cambrils	Shot down fighter (Sarrio)
8	Oblt.	Dieter Leicht	05.02.37	Málaga	Crashed with He.60
9	Inspek.	Ludwig Müller	31.12.38	Valls	Shot down fighter (Falco)
10	Gefr.	Siegfried Papendieck	09.04.37	Málaga	Bombing raid
11	Lt.z.See	Ernst Poeschel	01.01.39	At sea	Accident frozen wing
12	Oblt.	Carl Friedrich Printz	31.12.38	Valls	Shot down fighter (Falco)
13	Lt.	Otto Schmidt	31.12.38	Valls	Shot down fighter (Falco)
14	Lt.	Schöbel	01.01.39	At sea	Accident frozen wing
15	Uffz.	Kurt Werner	21.03.38	Cambrils	Shot down fighter (Sarrio)
16	Funker.	Zervas	01.01.39	At sea	Accident frozen wing
17	Lt.	Karl Zunker	21.03.38	Cambrils	Shot down fighter (Sarrio)

Appendix IV: Losses in Aircraft (Incomplete)

	Date	Aircraft N°	Place	Observations
1	19.12.36	He 59	At sea	Crew rescued by *Königsberg*. Probably lost.
2	05.02.37	He 59 (523)	Malaga	Crashed with He 60. Sunk by *Canarias*.
3	23.12.37	He 59	Benicarlo	Damaged by night fighter. Landed in sea and sunk.
4	13.01.38	He 59	Pollensa	Bad landing in thick fog. One dead. Written off.
5	28.01.38	He 59	Mahon	Ran out of fuel. Written off.
6	11.02.38	He 59	Pollensa	Destroyed by bad weather. Written off.
7	15.03.38	He 59 (529)	Vinaroz	Shot down by A/A train. Crew captured. Written off.
8	21.03.38	He 59	Cambrils	Shot down by night fighter (pilot Sgt. Sarrio).
9	30.04.38	He 59	Benicasim	Damaged by own bomb. Probably Written off.
10	01.08.38	He 59	S.C. Rapita	Damaged by A/A. Forced landing. Probably Written off
11	28.08.38	He 59 (532)	Pollensa	Bad landing, lost floats. Written off.
12	31.12.38	He 59 (538)	Valls	Shot down by night fighter (pilot Lt. Falco)
13	01.01.39	He 59	At sea	Accident, frozen wing. Lost.
14	05.01.39	He 59	Mediterranean	Damaged by enemy fighter. Probably written off.
15	06.03.39	He 59	Cabo Palos	Damaged by fighter. Sunk by cruiser *Canarias*.
16	22.03.39	He 59	Ibiza	Damaged engine. Bad landing. Written off.
17	22.03.39	He 59	Cartagena	Damaged by fighter. Probably written off.

Appendix V: Aircraft Numbers

Years 1936-37 HEINKEL HE 60

	Nº	Type	Observations
1	511	He 60	"*Terror of the Seas*"
2	512	He 60	"*Sea Beast*"
3	513	He 60	"*Sea Wolf*". Accident 22.04.37 (Huelva)
4	514	He 60	
5	515	He 60	Accident 19.03.37 (Malaga)

Years 1936-37 HEINKEL HE 59

	Nº	Type	Observations
1	521	He 59	Accident on 19.12.36. Probably Written off.
2	522	He 59	In Pollensa el 12.12.37.
3	523	He 59	Accident on 05.02.37 (Malaga). Sunk.
4	524	He 59	In Pollensa el 12.12.37.
5	525	He 59	In Pollensa el 12.12.37.
6	526	He 59	In Pollensa el 12.12.37.
7	528	He 59	Capt. Pombo; Capt. Lerdo; Lt. Ramos; 2nd Lt. Guillen.
8	529	He 59	Shot down 15.03.38 (Vinaroz). Crew captured.
9	530	He 59	In Pollensa el 12.12.37.

Year 1937 JUNKERS JU 52/3m (W)

	Nº	Type	Observations
1	527	Ju 52 (W)	

Years 1938-39 HEINKEL HE 59

	Nº	Type	Observations
10	531	He 59	Capt. Pombo. 2nd Lt. Guillen. Sgt. Julve.
11	532	He 59	Bad landing 28.08.38. (Pollensa)
12	533	He 59	(Undocumented). Written off.
13	534	He 59	Capt. Pombo. Lt. Ramos. 2nd Lt. Guillen. Sgt. Julve.
14	535	He 59	(Undocumented). Written off.
15	536	He 59	Capt. Pombo. Lt. Ramos. 2nd Lt. Guillen. Sgt. Julve.
16	537	He 59	Capt. Pombo. Lt. Ramos. 2nd Lt. Guillen. Sgt. Julve.
17	538	He 59	Shot down 31.12.38 (Valls)

18	539	He 59	Capt. Pombo. Lt. Corton. Sgt. Julve.
19	540	He 59	Capt. Pombo. Lt. Ramos. Lt. Corton. 2nd Lt. Guillen
20	541	He 59	Capt. Pombo. 2nd Lt. Guillen. Sgt. Julve.
21	542	He 59	Capt. Pombo. Lt. Ramos. Lt. Corton. 2nd Lt. Guillen
22	543	He 59	2nd Lt. Guillen. Sgt. Julve.
23	544	He 59	2nd Lt. Guillen. Sgt. Julve.
24	545	He 59	Capt. Pombo. Lt. Corton.
25	546	He 59	Lt. Corton. 2nd Lt. Guillen.
26	547	He 59	(Undocumented)
27	548	He 59	(Undocumented)

Appendix VI: Chronological List of Vessels Captured or Sunk by AS./88

Nº	Name	Date	Country	Tonnage (Gross)	Captured/Sunk
1	*Nuria Ramos*	31.01.37	Spain	2,783 tons.	C
2	*Delfín*	01.02.37	Spain	1,254 tons.	S
3	*Lancha 41*	30.07.37	Spain	15.73 tons.	S
4	*Edith*	13.08.37	Denmark	1,566 tons.	S
5	*Guecho*	30.09.37	Spain	3,276 tons.	S
6	*Oued-Mellah*	24.10.37	France	2,413 tons.	S
7	*Chasseur 91*	25.10.37	France	73 tons.	S
8	*Jean Weems*	30.10.37	Great Britain	2,349 tons.	S
9	*Alcira*	04.02.38	Great Britain	1,387 tons.	S
10	Unknown	25.02.38		250 tons.	S
11	*Cabo Tres Forcas*	26.02.38	Spain	2,265 tons.	S
12	*Isla de Menorca*	14.03.38	Spain	1,003 tons.	S
13	*San Silverio*	18.03.38	Spain	60 tons.	S
14	*V-13 Río Urumea*	07.04.38	Spain	276 tons.	S
15	*Dédalo*	22.04.38	Spain	9,900 tons.	S
16	Unknown	18.05.38			S
17	Unknown	22.05.38			S
18	*Thorpehall*	25.05.38	Great Britain	1,251 tons.	S

19	Unknown	27.05.38		1,500 tons.	S
20	*Nausicaa*	28.05.38	Greece	5,005 tons.	S
21	*El Djem*	29.05.38	France	2,575 tons.	S
22	*Penthames*	31.05.38	Great Britain	3,995 tons.	S
23	*Maryad*	04.06.38	Great Britain		S
24	*Frutero*	07.06.38	Spain	340 tons.	S
25	*Thorpehaven*	07.06.38	Great Britain	3,688 tons.	S
26	*English Tanker*	07.06.38	Great Britain	6,170 tons.	S
27	*Cala Fornells*	07.06.38	Spain	93 tons.	S
28	*Gandía*	07.06.38	Great Britain	316 tons.	S
29	*Pascual Flores*	08.06.38	Spain	169 tons.	S
30	*Isadora*	09.06.38	Great Britain	1,324 tons.	S
31	*Cala Portals*	09.06.38	Spain	130 tons.	S
32	*Brisbane*	13.06.38	France	4,004 tons.	S
33	*Thorpeness*	21.06.38	Great Britain	4,798 tons.	S
34	*Sunion*	22.06.38	Great Britain	3,054 tons.	S
35	Unknown	22.06.38			S
36	*Betis*	12.07.38	Spain	1,011 tons.	S
37	*Bodil*	21.07.38	Denmark	844 tons.	S
38	*Vicente*	24.07.38	Spain	543 tons.	S
39	*Antonio Matutes*	25.07.38	Spain	66 tons.	S
40	*Dellwyn*	26.07.38	Great Britain	1,451 tons.	S

41	*Lake Lugano*	07.08.38	Great Britain	2,120 tons.	S
42	*Campomanes*	15.08.38	Spain	6,276 tons.	S
43	*Eleni*	04.11.38	Cyprus	1,138 tons.	S
44	*Margaret Rose*	07.11.38	Great Britain		S
45	*Almería*	07.11.38	Spain	564 tons.	S
46	*D-171*	07.11.38	Spain		S
47	*D-173*	07.11.38	Spain		S
48	Unknown	08.11.38	Spain		S

Bibliography

Documents
The "Álvaro de Bazan" General Maritime Archive, Viso del Marques, Ciudad Real.
Central Naval Archive. Naval Headquarters, Madrid.
General Military Archive, Avila.
Spanish Civil War Archive, Salamanca.
Air Force Historical Archive, Castillo de Villaviciosa de Odon, Madrid.
Iberisa Archive, Madrid.
National Library Madrid.
Bundesarchiv Militararchiv, Freiburg (Germany).
Naval Staff Historical Service, Madrid.

Books:
ALPERT, Michael: *La guerra civil española en el mar*. Madrid, 1987.
ARIAS RAMOS, Raúl: *Legión Cóndor. Su historia 60 años después*. Madrid, 2000.
DÍAZ LORENZO, Juan Carlos: *Empresa naviera Elcano. Seis décadas de historia*. Madrid,
GARATE CORDOBA, José María: *Partes oficiales de guerra 1936-1939.Tomo I Ejército nacional*. y *Tomo II Ejército de la República*. Madrid, 1978.
GONZALEZ ECHEGARAY, Rafael: *La marina mercante y el tráfico marítimo en la guerra civil*. Madrid, 1977.
GONZALEZ HUIX, Francisco: *El asedio aéreo de Tarragona 1937-1939*. Tarragona, 1990.
GRETTON, Peter: The forgotten Factor. *The British Navy and the Spanish Civil War*. Madrid, 1984.
HERRERA ALONSO, Emilio: *Entre el añil y el cobalto. Los hidroaviones en la guerra de España*. Madrid, 1987.
LAUCK, Friedrich: *Der Lufttorpedo.Entwicklung und Technik in Deutschland 1915-1945*. München, 1981.
MOLINA FRANCO, Lucas; MANRIQUE GARCIA, José María: *Legión Cóndor. La historia olvidada*. Valladolid, 2000.
MORENO DE ALBORÁN y DE REYNA, Fernando y Salvador: *La guerra silenciosa y silenciada. Historia de la campaña naval durante la guerra de 1936-39*. Madrid, 1998.
PAZ DURÁN, José Luis: *28 meses a bordo del Canarias (1936-1939)*. La Coruña, 1991.
PUCHOL FRANCO, Miguel: *Bombardeos en Águilas*. Murcia,2003.
RIES, Carl; RING, Hans: *The Condor Legion. A History of the Luftwaffe in the Spanish Civil War. 1936-1939*. Pennsylvania, 1992.

SABATIER DE LACHADENÈDE, René: *La Marina francesa y la guerra civil de España (1936-1939)*. Madrid, 2000.

THIELE, Harold: *Luftwaffe Aerial Torpedo Aircraft and Operations in World War Two*. Sussex, 2004.

Magazines

O´DONNELL TORROBA, César: *Las pérdidas de buques mercantes republicanos causadas por hidroaviones de la Legión Cóndor durante la guerra civil española (1936-1939)*. Naval History Magazine Nº 43. Madrid.